Books by Archie J. Bahm:

Philosophy: An Introduction, 1953
What Makes Acts Right?, 1958
Philosophy of the Buddha, 1958
Tao Teh King, 1958
Logic for Beginners, 1960
Types of Intuition, 1961
Yoga: Union with the Ultimate, 1961
The World's Living Religions, 1964
Yoga for Business Executives, 1965
The Heart of Confucius, 1969
Bhagavat Gita: The Wisdom of Krishna, 1970
Polarity, Dialectic and Organicity, 1970
Ethics as a Behavioral Science, 1974
Metaphysics: An Introduction, 1974
Comparative Philosophy, 1977
The Specialist, 1977
The Philosopher's World Model, 1979
Axiology: The Science of Values, 1980
Ethics: The Science of Oughtness, 1980
Why Be Moral?, 1980
Directory of American Philosophers, 1992

Archie J. Bahm

$\mathcal{T}$he Heart of · Confucius ·

Interpretations of *Genuine Living* and *Great Wisdom*

with a foreword by Thomé H. Fang

and sixteen Ming-dynasty Confucian prints

ASIAN HUMANITIES PRESS

Berkeley

ASIAN HUMANITIES PRESS

Asian Humanities Press offers to the specialist and the general reader alike the best in new translations of major works and significant original contributions to enhance our understanding of Asian literature, religions, cultures and thought.

Library of Congress Cataloging-in-Publication Data

Bahm, Archie J.
    The heart of Confucius: interpretations of Genuine living and Great wisdom / Archie J. Bahm; with a foreword by Thomé H. Fang.
       p.   cm.
    Originally published: New York: Walker/Weatherhill, 1969.
    Includes bibliographical references.
    ISBN 0-87573-021-3 (paper)
    1. Chung yung. 2. Ta hsüeh. I. Confucius.
II. Chung yung. English. 1992. III. Ta hsüeh. English. 1992. IV. Title.
PL2473.Z7B34 1992
181'.09512—dc20   92—20720
                                      CIP

Printed in the United States of America

Contents

Foreword

W/hat Professor Archie J. Bahm offers in this invaluable book is not a literal translation but a lively, systematic interpretation of the two most basic Confucian classics. Writing for the thinking, inquiring layman rather than for the scholar and Orientalist, he at last makes Confucianism meaningful to the West.

He is to be congratulated for the success he has achieved in presenting a crucial phase of Confucian thought to the naturalistically tempered Western mind. With an unusual clearness of thought and expression, he demonstrates that the Confucian mode of thought, developed over two thousand years ago, can still enlighten the modern world in its search for ways of living peacefully and prosperously together. He also effectively explodes the myth that Confucianism is *per se* a conservative, reactionary weapon of the Establishment, when in actuality it has as much meaning for the modern revolutionary as for the powers that be.

I am sure, then, that this work will be widely appreciated by peoples of both East and West.

THOMÉ H. FANG

Department of Philosophy
Taiwan National University

A Note on the Illustrations

The thoughts of great thinkers often emerge from grappling with the problems confronting them in their own lives. Since glimpses of events in the life of Confucius may prove insightful, the present book is illustrated with scenes from his life. Although these scenes of remembered events are depicted as imagined by sixteenth-century artists, doubtless their reconstructions have captured something of the authentic spirit of the original happenings.

Illustrated biographies of Confucius have been popular in China for centuries. One of the best-loved, perhaps because of the rough yet charming quality of its woodblock-print illustrations, was a two-volume work printed during the Ming dynasty, in 1598, showing scenes from the lives of both Confucius and Mencius. It is from the thirty-nine prints in the Confucian volume, entitled *K'ung-fu-tzu sheng-chi t'u* (Footprints of the Great Sage), that the present illustrations have been taken.

The plates appear here in the same chronological

order as in the original volume. The perceptive reader will be able to draw his own parallels between events in Confucius' life and his philosophy. Each illustration is briefly described in words taken from the Chinese texts accompanying the original illustrations.

We gratefully acknowledge the permission granted by the Maeda Ikutoku Kai to photograph the volume in the Sonkei Bunko library, Tokyo, there catalogued under the Japanese title *Koshi seiseki-zu.*

The following is a list of the illustrations and the pages on which they appear: 1) Lauding Genuine Living, 16–17; 2) Confucius' mother, 24–25; 3) A well-mannered child, 32–33; 4) Guarding a granary, 40–41; 5) Overseeing fields, 48–49; 6) Playing the lute, 56–57; 7) Visiting Lao Tzu, 72–73; 8) Prime Minister of Lu, 80–81; 9) The king's concubines, 88–89; 10) Treated like a vagabond, 96–97; 11) An interrupted journey, 104–5; 12) Questing the recluses, 112–13; 13) An omen from the stars, 120–21; 14) One week before death, 132–33; 15) The mourning disciples, 140–41; and 16) Posthumous honors, 148–49.

The Heart of Confucius

Introduction

Confucius is, without doubt the most famous, and the most influential, philosopher in the history of China. Indeed, he may be counted as one of the greatest in the history of mankind. He is also one of the earliest, since he lived during that great century, the sixth B.C., when Gotama, the Buddha; Mahavira, the Jain; and Lao Tzu, the Taoist, also flourished.

The ideas associated with his name have had a double significance in shaping the history of human civilization. First, they symbolize, better than any others, the ideals which have pervaded Chinese culture throughout most of its history and have molded Chinese minds and the consequent course of social, political, economic, religious, scientific, and technological developments in China. Secondly, and in the long run perhaps more importantly, these ideas have already contributed somewhat to philosophies in other cultures and promise to play a determining role in the world culture which is now emerging.

Those of us who are concerned about the shape of the future owe it to ourselves to understand these great ideas which promise to become ingredients in the mentality of mankind. To fail to understand the ideas attributed to Confucius is to remain deficient regarding something fundamental in human culture.

We leave to others the tasks of exploring problems of authenticity, varying versions purporting to transmit the views of Confucius, and shifts in interpretations of calligraphic symbols in different eras, and opposing schools of thought. Here we are concerned with the ideas themselves, i.e., the persisting opinions which have functioned effectively, rather than with details of who, precisely, thought of them first. The following interpretation of two works attributed, directly or indirectly, to Confucius involves a deliberate attempt to capture and depict a consistent system of ideas which is, at once, faithful to historical reality, cogently self-integrated (a system gestalt), and true to living experience of men today and tomorrow.

The two short works presented here are selected mainly because they summarize, both systematically and succinctly, the central ideas expounded by Confucius. The more famous *Lun Yu* or *Analects,* sometimes referred to as *Aphorisms,* consists of a miscellaneous collection of scattered remarks and disconnected stories, often leaving the reader puzzled as to whether

Confucius had a unified core of teachings. These two reinforce each other, and repetition of ideas tends to press home the persistence with which he maintained a foundational, intuitive simplicity underlying his profound wisdom. *Genuine Living, Great Wisdom,* and the *Analects,* together with a work attributed to his follower Mencius, *Meng-tzu,* constitute the classical "four books." These supplement the older, perhaps more sacred, "five books" containing ancient records with which Confucius worked, or reworked, namely, the *Shu-ching (Shu-King)* or *Book of Historical Documents,* the *Shih-ching (Shih-King)* or *Book of Ancient Poems,* the *I Ching (Yi King)* or *Book of Changes,* the *Li-chi (Li-Ki)* or *Book of Rites and Ancient Ceremonies* (within which *Genuine Living* itself is embedded as Chapter XXXI), and *Ch'un Ch'iu* or *Spring and Autumn,* being the annals of the state of Lu. The thorough student of Confucius has a plenty of material with which to pursue his studies. Our purpose is to provide a quick, clear introduction for the nonspecialist.

The best way to introduce the philosophy of Confucius, I believe, is to develop first the ancient ideas of *tao* and *teh* and of *yang* and *yin* as these are presented in the *Tao Teh King (Tao Te Ching),* a work traditionally attributed to Lao Tzu. Difficulties in translating this work into readable English, and the existence of popular translations clearly exhibiting

Confucius lauds the
lofty and wise principles
of Genuine Living,
handed down from the
ancient sages, as har-
monizing with the
laws of nature exem-
plified in the lives
of wise kings and
available to all, every-
where, any time.

Buddhistic and Christian biases, provoked me into preparing my own edition, interpreting the *Tao Teh King* as the *Book of Nature and Intelligence* (Ungar, N.Y., 1958). The quotations contained in the following remarks are from this edition.

Tao   *Tao* is Nature. By "Nature" is meant the whole universe, including everything within the universe, as it proceeds on its course without interruption. *Tao* is the way. It is the way of Nature which proceeds through comings and goings, beginnings and endings. The way of Nature can be observed in the procession of the seasons. In spring, seeds sprout, plants start growing, trees turn green, and flowers blossom. In summer, plants grow up, tree leaves mature, flowers wilt under the blaze of the sun, and new seeds begin to take shape. In autumn, the fruit and grain ripen while leaves fall, and plants dry up, turn brown, and wither. In winter, plants die and begin to decay; but winter moisture penetrates the seeds which have fallen to the ground, readying them for spring sprouting. The way of Nature is observed also in the path of the sun, which rises in the morning, ascends to the highest heaven at noon, and then descends through the afternoon into evening, thereafter remaining hidden in the dark during the night. The way of Nature is revealed in the course of human life, as when an infant is born, grows through childhood, youth, middle age, maturity, and old age, and finally dies. This way of Nature is evident to everyone who cares to observe it. And it is this way which, according to both Lao Tzu and Confucius, serves as the pattern, indeed as the ideal, which men, if they are wise, will seek to emulate.

Nature consists of natures. The universe consists of beings, such as men and animals, plants and trees, mountains and lakes, wind and water. Each of these different beings has its own nature. And each naturally follows its own nature, just as Nature does. The universal *Tao* consists of many *tao*'s, and every such *tao* also has a natural way of its own to follow, from its beginning, through its early stages, through its maturing stages, until it comes finally to its own end in its own way. Nature is good; and each nature is good, at least so long as it pursues its own course without being interfered with by other natures or without imposing its own nature upon others. Now, curiously enough, some beings do impose themselves upon others and are imposed upon by others. Some, especially men, also try to modify their own natures, by trying to live a longer life than their own nature provides for them. It is this tendency of men to meddle with Nature by meddling with their own natures, e.g., by becoming too aggressive or ambitious or too submissive or lazy, which gives rise to the notion that some have an ability to live their lives more naturally while others lack such ability.

Teh   *Teh* is the ability of anything to follow its own nature. It is the power of Nature to be natural, and it is the power of each particular being to behave in accordance with its own nature. Now Nature never behaves unnaturally, except, perhaps, through the unnatural behavior of particular beings, especially men, who, unfortunately, have a tendency to become artificial. Now art is anything which is man-made, and artificiality characterizes man's way of making himself different, of modifying his nature, or of deviating from his own best way. For example, it is natural to eat until one's hunger is satisfied; but some men prepare foods so tasty that they want to eat more even after they have had enough. Some men fast, for whatever reason, not just to make fever subside or to lose excessive weight, but because they believe asceticism is somehow inherently virtuous. To overeat and to undereat are both ways of deviating from what is best. Since some deviate and some do not, *teh* names the ability of those who succeed in not deviating from their natural way. "Whatever acts unnaturally will come to an unnatural finish" (p. 34). "Those too eager for activity soon become fatigued. When they exhaust their vigor, they age quickly. Such impatience is against Nature. What is against Nature dies young" (pp. 51–52).

Another way of being artificial, in addition to deviating from one's own way, is to cause others to deviate from their natures. That is, whenever one person imposes his ideas, plans, or schemes upon others, he forces them to follow his way rather than their own way. For example, that horses should have hoofs is natural, but that they should have harnesses is artificial. "When what is natural prevails in human affairs, horses forced to train for racing are returned to the fertile pastures. When artificiality prevails in human affairs, horses are trained for war and are restricted to walled enclosures. There is no greater evil than desiring to change others. There is no greater misfortune than desiring to change oneself" (p. 45).

Lao Tzu, in drawing out the implications of his naturalism for government, reached anarchistic conclusions. Although he did not advocate hermitic existence, apparently, since he idealized living in a rural community where people seldom bothered to visit their neighbors, he did urge avoidance of unnecessary association. When *teh* prevails in the lives of men, there are no governors or tax collectors. "Those who make their living by collecting taxes cause the people to starve; when the people starve, the tax collectors, having no one to tax, starve also. Those who govern people make them discontented with being controlled and therefore cause them to be uncontrollable" (p. 65). "The more laws are enacted and taxes assessed, the greater the number of law breakers and tax evaders. . . . When government governs little, people are happy. When government governs much, people are miserable" (p. 53). "When opposing armies meet for open battle, he who runs away to hide is the one who wins" (p. 62). So, al-although Lao Tzu was not completely antisocial, the burden of his naturalism was to avoid the artificial-ities which result from association. "If one remains silent and keeps to himself, he will not fail to fulfill his life; but if he gives advice and meddles in the af-fairs of others, he invites trouble" (p. 49).

The idea of life fulfillment through associating with others, first in family life, then in community life, and then in national life, was left for Confucius to develop. Yet even here, Lao Tzu's views were in agreement with those of Confucius regarding the best way of teaching, i.e., by example: "One's own individual life serves as an example for other indi-viduals. One's family serves as a model for other families. One's community serves as a standard for other communities. One's state serves as a measure for other states. And one's country serves as an ideal for all countries" (pp. 50–51). Lao Tzu's philosophy was positive, not negative, in its basic intent: "Nature sustains itself through three precious principles, which one does well to embrace and follow. These are gentleness, frugality, and humility. When one is gentle, he has no fear of retaliation. When one is frugal, he can afford to be generous. When one is humble, no one challenges his leadership" (p. 60). "Simply be yourself. Act naturally. Refrain from self-assertiveness. Avoid covetousness" (p. 25). Yet, when compared with the ideals and emphases developed by Confucius, the social philosophy of Lao Tzu appears to be inadequate, and even quite immature, as we shall see.

Yang and Yin   The beginnings and endings of all things in Nature are referred to as *yang* and *yin*. *Yang* and *yin* are opposites. "The tendency toward opposition is ever present. Opposition is the source of all growth. . . . The principle of opposition is inherent in Nature, so oppositeness will continue forever, no matter how many opposites may come and go. The principle of initiation *(yang)* persists; and the principle of completion *(yin)* continues also" (p. 15). "Opposites are not sympathetic to each other. Each one of many kinds of opposites acts as if it could get along without its complement. But Nature treats opposites impartially, dealing with each of every pair of

According to a family legend, Confucius' pregnant mother, hoping for a son, prayed to Mount Ni, promising that if her child was a male, she would name him after the mountain. Hence Confucius' name—Chung-ni.

opposites with the same indifference. And an intelligent man will regard opposites in the same manner"
(p. 14). "All things are impregnated by two alternating tendencies, the tendency toward completion and
the tendency toward initiation, which, acting together, complement each other" (p. 43). "Ultimate
reality involves initiation of growth, initiation of
growth involves completion of growth, and completion of growth involves returning to that whence it
came" (p. 30). And "each thing which grows and
develops to the fullness of its own nature completes its
course by declining again in a manner inherently
determined by its own nature" (p. 23). From these
generalizations there follows a conclusion which men
only reluctantly draw: "It is natural for men to be
born and to die" (p. 47).

The humanistic Confucius accepts these views of
the naturalistic Lao Tzu. But Confucius observes
that it is also natural for men to be social and that
the principles of initiation and completion *(yang* and
yin) permeate human association also in ways which
are obvious to anyone who takes the trouble to recognize them.

Yi   Although the philosophy of Confucius has been
organized in many different ways, a most efficient
way to summarize his teachings is to interpret the

meanings of four interrelated terms which have no exact equivalents in English. These four are *yi, jen, li,* and *chih.*

Yi (i) symbolizes the best way of doing things. What is this best way? Lao Tzu had already stated that whatever is natural is good, that each thing has its own nature, and that what is best for it comes about naturally when it does not deviate from its own way. The wise man neither deviates from the way inherent in his own inner nature nor causes others to stray from the ways of their own inner natures. Both Lao Tzu and Confucius agreed on this point. When a *tao* has *teh,* then *yi* prevails. When *yi* prevails, then a *tao* has *teh.* "It is by self-activity that all things fulfill themselves" (p. 40). "If there were no self-activity, life would cease. If self-activity did not govern, then disruption would set in" (p. 41). "By letting each thing act in accordance with its own nature, everything that needs to be done gets done" (p. 46). This is the best way of doing things.

Knowing *yi* not only entails understanding how undisturbed self-activity leads to fulfillment of each being but also provides insight into what is best in social relations. "The intelligent man expresses his beneficence to other men by accepting each man's way as best for himself. And he performs the same service for all other beings, for he willingly recognizes that, by following its own nature, each thing does the

best that can be done for it" (p. 31). "Being intelligent, he knows that each thing has a nature which
is able to take care of itself. Knowing this, he is willing that each thing follow its own course. Being willing to let each thing follow its own course, he is gracious" (p. 23). Thus, in the writings attributed to Lao
Tzu, we find Confucius' *yi,* including a sound naturalistic foundation for his socialistic conception of
jen, already clearly described.

Jen   But the ways in which *jen* was further studiously
elaborated by Confucius yield ideals which, popu-
larly at least, have come to seem most typically characteristic of his thought. *Jen* is good will. That is, it
is a willingness to do what is best socially. The basis
of this view can also be stated in the words of Lao
Tzu: "The intelligent man is not willful. He accepts
what others will for themselves as his will for them"
(p. 47). However, when persons actually interdepend
intimately, as do a mother and her child, they have
mutual interests as well as their own separate self-
activity. Since an infant cannot survive without food
from its mother's breast, and since a mother, having
produced milk, needs the relief which comes when
her child suckles, the self-activity of each involves
cooperation with the other. Here is a basic example
of natural social cooperation. Associating with her

child is a natural part of a mother's self-activity, just as associating with its mother is a natural part of a child's self-activity. Hence, such social activity is not unnatural. It is not artificial. In such social cooperation, neither imposes his will upon the other, neither meddles with, or tries to change the nature of, the other, and neither deviates from his own nature in providing for the other what the other needs in pursuit of his own self-activity. For Confucius, association is natural, and when it occurs naturally, i.e., in such a way that two persons mutually support each other's nature, all goes well. In this way, *jen* is embodied in the lives of both.

By studying the nature of human association, in his own community, in the courts of other kingdoms, and in records of the past, Confucius observed a basic principle in constant operation, namely, the principle of reciprocity. This principle, whereby persons tend to act in relation to others as others act in relation to them, is itself a more specific exemplification of the *yin-yang* principle of *Tao*, whereby each occasion on which some action is initiated *(yang)* by, or in, a *tao* is followed naturally by some reaction which supplements and completes the action *(yin)*. The *yin-yang* principle, which pervades all of Nature and determines the course of all particular natures, manifests itself in social interaction as the principle of reciprocity. When an infant cries because he is hungry, he thus initiates action *(yang)*, and when the mother responds by suckling the child and satisfying his hunger, she completes the action *(yin)* which the infant's hunger started. But the principle of reciprocity, when it operates in more complex human associations, may be observed as manifesting more intricate and subtle aspects. *Jen,* good will, involves willingness to interact and cooperate reciprocally for mutual benefit. And *jen,* as an attitude embodied in one person, tends to elicit reciprocation of a *jen* attitude in other persons. Love of a mother for her child tends to generate love by a child for its mother.

One may question whether the principle, which works so obviously in a mother-child relationship, also operates in other associations, such as those we find in business and politics and war. Confucius' conclusion, drawn from his various studies, was that it does operate, although, since people do differ in their natures, inner and outer, these differences must be taken into consideration when interpreting the way it operates.

That it does so work, he emphasized by summarizing five kinds of relationships which may then be taken as illustrative of all human relationships. The five: those between parent and child, husband and wife, older brother and younger brother, ruler and subject, and friend and friend. These five were perhaps among the most obvious in the family and courtly life of Confucius' own time. In a Chinese patriarchal family, the father was primarily responsible for family welfare, and the eldest son tended to receive the father's first attention, since it was the eldest son who, after the father's death, would become the most responsible person in the family. Hence, the mutual respect of a father for his son and of a son for his father was regarded as the cornerstone of the family system. We misunderstand what is translated into English as "filial piety" if we fail to grasp its significance as the foundational example of *jen* wherein the respect which a father has for his son and successor is duly recognized and reciprocated. Such reciprocation is complicated by the fact that it turns out to be two-directional; the son not only needs to recognize the father's good will and develop good will toward his father but also to recognize the naturalness and need for developing good will toward his own sons when the time comes for him to have sons. A son's good will toward his own sons serves as a part of the expression of his good will toward his father.

Subtleties involved in the operation of the principle of reciprocity between different kinds of people may be observed as inherent in this foundational example. What is best for a son? Father and son are different. Should a father treat his son as an equal, i.e., as if he also were already a father? No, for a son is

According to the Book of History, Confucius became so interested in good manners even as a child that he paid great attention to them even while playing.

not already a father. Rather, he should treat his son as he would like to be treated if he were his son. And a son should treat his father as he would like to be treated if he were his father, or as he would like to be treated when he becomes a father. For Confucius, the principle is not strictly equalitarian. People who are unequal should not mistakenly treat each other as if they were equals. Confucius taught "discriminating love," i.e., good will toward others which takes into account the actual differences involved in their inner natures and also their social positions.

After discovering how discriminatingly this principle of reciprocity needs to be used in accounting for the significant and subtle differences between father and son, we are now in a position to see how, and why, it may be observed operating also in all other kinds of association. The mother-daughter, and mother-son, relationships have a pattern closely similar to that of father and son. The husband-wife relationship perhaps next most obviously requires discriminating awareness of differences. For a husband should not treat his wife as if she were his husband; first of all, she is a woman, not a man, and so wishes to be regarded as a woman with a female, not a male, nature; and she is a wife, having both privileges and duties which inhere in that social position, so she wishes to be treated as a wife, not as a sister, not as a passing entertainer, not as a child. So, only when a husband treats his wife as he would like to be treated if he were his wife, does he deserve, according to the principle of reciprocity, to be treated by his wife as she would like to be treated if she were her husband. Elder-brother and younger-brother relationships had a special significance in the ancient system which has disappeared in American life. But the problems encountered in ruler-subject relationships recur somewhat similarly in official-citizen relations, and in friend-friend relationships, which persist everywhere, and may serve as a basis for extrapolating ways of discriminating differences between stranger and stranger as well as enemy and enemy.

Confucius did not assert that the principle of reciprocity works unerringly. Rather, like Lao Tzu's sermonizing about men lacking *teh,* the central burden of Confucius' writings seems to be that men too often fail to be genuine (i.e., lack *chung*), and this is the very reason for his becoming a teacher, a writer, and, for a while, an administrator. Confucius did not expect that many people would succeed in perfecting *jen,* for he complained about his own deficiencies: "The nature of a wise man includes four achievements, none of which have I attained: to appreciate my father as I wish my son to appreciate me . . . to serve my superior officers as I desire my subordinate officials to serve me . . . to treat my elder brother in the same way I would expect my younger brother to treat me . . . to be as considerate of friends as I would like to have my friends be considerate of me" *(Chung Yung*, XIII*)*. Having discovered that embodying *jen*, including a willingness to discriminatingly treat others reciprocally, is a part of the best ways of doing things socially *(yi)*, he had to describe it as an ideal and to recommend it to all who would live wisely and happily and more fully in accordance with their own social natures.

Inherent in the functioning of the principle of reciprocity is another principle, namely, *hsin* or sincerity. This is so important that some regard it, along with *yi, jen, li,* and *chih,* as a fifth characteristic of the wise man. Sincerity is necessary in dealing with others, because when you are not sincere with others then the most that you can expect from them, according to the principle of reciprocity, is that they will be insincere with you. Merely pretended good will toward others will result in merely pretended good will to you. Such pretension is deceitful. Deceit begets deceit, distrust, and fear. Hence, having *hsin*, sincerity in dealings with others—one's son, one's wife, one's brothers and sisters, one's subjects, and one's friends and even enemies—is essential to wisdom, because it is inherent in the nature of *jen*.

Finally, Confucius' conception of *jen* appears to involve two other elements, sympathetic insight and sympathy, two items not needed, or rather not something that needs to be kept in mind, according to the philosophy of Lao Tzu. For Lao Tzu, having general knowledge that each thing has its own nature and that, if left alone, it will fulfill that nature in the way that is best for it, is sufficient. One need merely refrain from meddling in the lives of others and all will go well. He would not have objected to the assertion that the principle of reciprocity often works, i.e., if you do not disturb me, then I will not disturb you. But the effort involved in trying to gain insight into the natures of others, which is required when one seeks to treat another as he would like to be treated if he were that other person, seems missing from the ideals stated by Lao Tzu. But, for Confucius, apparently, sympathetic insight is not enough. The principle of reciprocity requires also sympathy. Although there are limits to which one person can understand and share his feelings, the willingness to do so, and the sincere attempt to do so, as much as one can, is surely a fundamental part of *jen*.

Some Westerners, including Christians, observing that the Confucian formulation of advice based on the principle of reciprocity is stated in negative terms, "Do not . . . ," while Jesus' formulation is stated positively, "Do unto others . . . ," have concluded that the positive statement is superior. While discussing this issue with Chinese friends in Taiwan, I learned their reasons for thinking that the negative statement is really superior. These reasons are inherent in the Taoistic ideal of *teh,* namely, that one who has *teh* will neither deviate from nature's way for his own life nor try to interfere with nature's way for the lives of others. To "do to others," if that means taking the initiative, is a form of "meddling." Hence, the most appropriate way of formulating ideals regarding reciprocal behavior is to state, as Confucius did, that one should "not do to others what you would not have others do to you." Western ideals, growing out of Hebraic heritage, in which the will of God and the wills of men play a dominant role, tend to be stated in terms of willful, even aggressive, assertion, rather than in terms of willing, permissive, even submissive, acceptance. Thus, although it is easy to make too much of the distinction, there are bases in the Hebraic-Christian-Islamic traditions which justify preference for positive formulation and equally substantial bases in the Taoist-Confucian tradition which justify preference for a negative formulation. Actually, reciprocality involves both positive and negative aspects; for no matter how one prefers to state his ideals, the need for both *doing* and *doing not* recurs so frequently that dogmatic insistence on preference for either an exclusively positive or negative formulation soon proves itself to be inadequate. One may require great effort of will to "do not" on some occasions, whereas at other times the need for "doing" occurs quite spontaneously, as when an infant seeks the breast of a ready mother.

Jen, then, is a very profound, complex, and subtle ideal. Based in the Taoistic ideas of *Tao* and *tao*'s, Nature and natures, each of which self-actively tends to realize its own good naturally, through the ever present alternating *yin-yang* tendencies, it incorporates the ideal of *teh,* nondeviation from Nature's way in oneself and in relation with others. But it extends these ideals by recognizing that the mother-child and husband-wife associations and, by extension, all other kinds of association, are also natural and involve certain natural principles inherent in the reciprocating tendencies in human nature, including sincerity, the need for sympathetic insight and sympathy, and confidence, justified by experience, and that attentive good will toward others is part of what is needed to assure wholesome and happy self-realization. For Confucius, *jen* is inherently involved in *yi,* the best way of doing things.

Li *Li* is propriety. Yet it is much more than simply the socially proper ways of behaving. Confucius regarded it as the appropriate manner of overt behavior needed to express one's inner thoughts or intentions. Not only is there a best way of doing things in the sense that each thing lives in accordance with its own

Reports tell that, when Confucius began his career in Lu as a guardian of the granary, he practiced the principle that every official should do his duty to the best of his ability no matter what his capacity or learning.

inner nature *(yi)*, but also there is a best way of doing things in one's relations with others so that they
will not mistake one's intentions *(li)*. The best way
to express good will *(jen)* is in such a manner that
others will not misunderstand it; hence one's outer
forms of expression should be correlative with one's
inner nature, at least if his intentions are sincere.
Hence, *yi, jen,* and *hsin* require *li.*

Now it may not always be possible to convey
clearly what one's attitude toward another is. But by
studying the customs of different families and of different kingdoms, past and present, Confucius concluded that those behavior patterns adopted by the
most successful families were doubtless the best; and
so, in becoming a teacher, he himself taught that certain forms of behavior were the best ways to give
expression to one's good intentions. When such forms,
which constitute what we have come to call "etiquette," are agreed upon by the family or community, then they are available for one's use. One
who fails to make use of them, and thereby reduces
his chances of being understood, is foolish indeed.

Unfortunately, once the forms of etiquette have
been established, deceivers may utilize them also.
After one has been deceived by trusting the behavior
of someone who has used them, he is less likely to
trust them. Furthermore, when anxious parents
teach their children to conform to customary modes

of behavior before the children comprehend the significance of, and need for, such manners, the children tend to feel forced into ways of behaving which are external to their nature. To learn the customary forms of external behavior without understanding their inner significance is artificial, not natural. To learn the social proprieties without learning why they are appropriate is to be misinformed. For Confucius, *li* consists in only those forms of propriety which are appropriate. Without appropriateness, propriety is false. Both Lao Tzu and Confucius advocated shunning the artificial. Lao Tzu regarded all external formalities as artificial. But Confucius viewed as artificial any manner of behaving which failed to express one's true intentions. When one's external forms do not correctly reveal one's internal attitudes, one's behavior is formalistic. Confucius, thus, advised against formalism. *Hsin,* sincerity, requires that one be not formalistic. Although, doubtless, the continued indoctrination, generation after generation and century after century, of the ideals recommended by Confucius gave rise to, and perpetuated, much that is formalistic, too many have forgotten that antiformalism is itself an inherent part of the teachings of Confucius.

This antiformalistic doctine was also stated explicitly in what is often translated into English as "rectification of names." Again in the interest of avoiding misunderstanding in social relations, Confucius argued that names and natures should be correlated. When things are alike, they should be called by the same name. When things are different, they should be called by different names. When people are alike because they all belong to the same family, they should have the same family name. When they differ from all others in being individuals, they should also have individual names. When two children are alike in being children, they should both be called "children." But when two persons differ, as when one is a father and the other is his son, then they should be called "father" and "son" respectively. To call a son a father when he is not a father is to misname him. Each different kind of thing (shoe, bowl, door), each different member of a family (wife, eldest son, youngest daughter, third cousin), and each kind of officer (king, minister, guard) should have its own name.

Artificiality, and insincerity, in the use of names can be avoided only if both of the two sides of the principle of rectification of names are respected. On the one hand, the right name should be used to distinguish an actual nature or office. On the other, a person, especially an officer, should endeavor to live and behave in accordance with the name of his position and office. To call a wife a boy, or to call a ruler a clown, is to misuse names. But also, when a person fails to live up to his name, he is misusing names. If a ruler ceases to be concerned about the welfare of his people, he no longer acts like a ruler and so may properly be deposed because he fails to live up to his name. If a wife neglects her husband and distributes her favors to other men, she no longer acts like a wife and so may properly be divorced because she fails to live up to her name. The doctrine of the rectification of names is, thus, one clear expression of Confucius' antiformalism. *Li*, propriety, properly understood, involves appropriateness. And *li*, so understood, is thus involved in *yi*, the best way of doing things, and in *jen*, the expression of good will which people sincerely have for one another.

One further controversial item in interpreting Confucius should be mentioned. Although relatively minor, it may serve as a clue to misunderstandings by both blind followers and prejudiced critics. Confucius' concern for intricate analyses of factors in association, including details of etiquette *(li)*, led him, in studying the customs and rituals of historical and contemporary court life, to cite examples of good forms of conduct. In response to questioning by his pupils, he offered definite suggestions for some kinds of behavior which could be carried out even down to some very fine points. This characteristic of his teaching has been called, in English, "punctiliousness." After formalistic interpretations of his sayings by uncritical followers came to prevail, many insisted upon carrying out his "instructions" to the last letter even though following them became obviously absurd to others. And critics, both those from opposing schools of thought in China and those from other countries looking for excuses to justify the prejudice that their own culture was superior to that of the Chinese, seized upon such formalism and its punctilious performance as evidence of Confucian inferiority.

However, interest in meticulous performance of codes of behavior which have been discovered to be best may flow from a sympathetic interpretation of the principle of reciprocity as a fundamental ingredient in *jen*. In giving external expression to one's inner feelings in situations of deep concern, such as in the death of a beloved parent, desire to do exactly the right thing so as to assure fullest expression of one's inner grief leads naturally to doing precisely what is socially appropriate. If the naturalness of such desire is not obvious to the reader, appeal to an analogy may be useful here. Among our own ideals, in the use of scientific techniques, for example, we require precision in our laboratories and perfect cleanliness in our hospital operating rooms. In generating our own ideal of precision in measurement and meticulousness in procedures, we too demand "punctiliousness." Should we allow the fact that formalism developed and that critics rightly attacked punctilious performance of obsolete customs to obscure Confucius' own condemnation of artificiality while offering advice about how meticulously one may pursue his manner of expression toward others if he wishes to have that same manner, and meticulousness, manifest in the behavior of others toward him?

Chih *Chih* is wisdom. Wisdom involves 1) understanding *yi*, i.e., that acting naturally is the best way of doing things; 2) having *jen*, i.e., embodying genuine good will sincerely; 3) knowing and conscientiously practicing *li*, i.e., acting in a manner which always appropriately expresses one's inner attitudes; and also 4) habitually embodying in one's attitude and actions a complete willingness to act in accordance with *yi*, *jen*, and *li*. It is this unreserved commitment to wanting and doing whatever is best which constitutes *chih*. One who has *chih* faces life's problems willingly and responds to the needs for his services to others unquestioningly. This does not mean that he raises no questions, but only that he raises no questions about his willingness to do what the situation requires of him. This does mean that he is committed completely to intellectual and moral

It is said that even when Confucius served as an overseer of the fields, he did not consider the post so low that he failed to put forth his best efforts in performing its duties.

honesty. Wisdom is not a momentary affair, but is a persisting tendency to respond, both genuinely and willingly, to each personal and social task as it comes.

The ideal, *chih,* may be referred to or expressed in different ways. The titles of the two following works serve as illustrations. *Ta Hsueh,* which I interpret as "Great Wisdom," expresses an attitude of appreciation and admiration for the greatness of the teaching. "Wisdom" (i.e., *hsueh*) refers more to the ideals as taught or learned, whereas "wisdom" *(chih)* designates embodiment of such ideals in habitual commitment. *Chung Yung,* which I interpret as "Genuine Living," includes both nondeviant attitude and behavior and also the enduring character of commitment to such nondeviation. Thus one cannot achieve *chih* without incorporating *chung* in such living. But *chung* is a term rich in its own subtle connotations, which need further exploration.

Chung   Without hoping to exhaust the full meaning of *chung,* we will examine its relation to four other terms with which it is associated in the works of Confucius.

When associated with *yung,* as in the title *Chung Yung,* it means undeviating behavior, while *yung* means enduring. *Chung yung* is behavior that is enduringly undeviating. This is genuine living. Those who deviate, who lean toward either one side or the other of the way *(tao)*, lack *teh*. They lack genuineness. They fail to adhere to their true nature. Some attain *chung*, but do not maintain it for long. They lack *yung*, steadfastness, constancy, persistence, or strength to continue virtuously. One whose living embodies *yung* as well as *chung* behaves in such a way that we are warranted in having confidence in his reliability. To translate *chung yung* as "mean-in-action" is to fail to connote clearly how basic the idea of non-deviation is to the notion of *tao* and how necessary it is for genuine living, on the one hand, and the idea of the sturdiness and perpetuation of such tendency toward nondeviation on the other. *Chung* is no mere mean between extremes. As deviation begins, *chung* declines. *Chung* is prior to extremes; extremes of deviation exist only in the absence of *chung*. *Chung* exists only as the absence of extremes, not as a mean between them.

When *chung* is contrasted with *ho*, as in the opening section of the *Chung Yung*, *chung* means "true," i.e., living in accordance with one's true nature, whereas *ho* means "true together," i.e., where two or more persons are living together in such a way that both are living in accordance with their true natures. Hence, I have rendered *chung* as "one's genuine personal nature" and *ho* as "one's genuine social nature." *Ho* consists in two or more persons living

together harmoniously. As the text makes clear, Confucius believed that one could not embody *chung* completely without *ho,* just as *ho* cannot exist without
each person's embodying *chung.* Thomé H. Fang,
commenting on my proposed interpretation of *chung*
as "one's true individual nature" or "one's genuinely
intrinsic nature," for purposes of contrasing it with
man's additional social nature, remarked: "The same
Chinese character for *chung* has different meanings
attached to it. If used predicatively and pronounced
in the third pitch, it designates 1) the inner essence
of anything, 2) the middle part of any well-balanced
state of affairs, 3) the center of all circumstances, and
4) a metaphysical principle of axiological perfection.
At this juncture, the substantive use should be emphasized." *Ho* involves two substantive persons each
living genuinely, i.e., in accordance with his own
personal nature, but in such a way that each finds
his own self-realization partly in, through, and in a
way dependent upon, the genuine self-realization
of the other.

When *chung* is differentiated from *shu,* the first is
positive, the second negative. *Chung* is positive in the
sense that one does follow his own nature. *Shu,* like
the opposite side of the same coin, is negative in the
sense of not deviating from one's own nature. Socially, *chung* is positive in the sense of wanting for
others what is best for themselves, while *shu* is nega-

tive in the sense of refraining from wanting for others what is not best for them. Fung Yu-lan, in his *Short History of Chinese Philosophy* (p. 43), illustrates the difference by citing different formulations of the principle of reciprocity: "Do to others what you would like to have them do to you" is positive, exemplifying *chung*. "Do not do to others what you would not like to have them do to you" is negative, exemplifying *shu*.

When compared with *hsin*, sincerity in dealing with others, *chung* includes *hsin*. Without *hsin* there can be no *chung*, for Confucius, because there can be no *chung* without *ho*, two or more persons living in genuine harmony together, and such genuine harmony is impossible without *hsin*.

Conclusion   *Chung* cannot exist without knowing *yi*, the best way of doing things; without having *jen*, good will toward others; without knowing and practicing *li*, appropriately manifesting externally one's true personal intentions; and without beginning to achieve *chih*, habitual willingness to live according to *yi*, *jen*, and *li*. One may have *chung* without completely achieving *chih*, for *chih*, wisdom, is an ideal to be achieved. But *chung* involves both a willingness to achieve it and one's best efforts toward achievement. Thus, in sum, *chung yung* is another, even more succinct, way of signifying a life endeavoring to embody *yi, jen, li,* and *chih.* For Confucius, without *chung yung,* another name for genuine living, one fails to fully embody *yi, jen, li,* and *chih.*

At the risk of stretching what is meant by the foregoing terms too far, I suggest that some may find the ideas of Confucius somewhat more congenial if I depict them in terms of a loose analogy. The terms "science," "ethics," "morality," and "religion" have many meanings, and whatever they mean today may have only some small similarity to what Confucius had in mind. Yet, there appears to be a kind of similarity which may prove interesting to some readers.

The task of knowing *yi,* the way nature operates, is allotted to scientists today. Their function is to understand the laws of nature, or nature's way; and having done this, they present us with knowledge of how nature operates and of how, consequently, we should best conduct ourselves if we would utilize nature's providence in living out our own lives. The work of scientists is incomplete until they understand also how men behave in society, and which kinds of social organizations best serve the needs of men. History and anthropology, which study past forms of social conduct, and sociology and social psychology, which study interpersonal behavior patterns and processes, all serve to help us understand what are the best ways of doing things.

The task of understanding a person's views about the nature of good and evil, his intentions, his free will, his willingness or unwillingness to do what is best for him, and the feelings of duty, obligation, and justice, are all part of what today we call "ethics." In a sense, the central problem facing an ethicist is that of understanding *jen.* To what extent is it essential to the nature and welfare of each human being to want what is best for others as well as for himself? The attempt to understand the role of good will toward others, and how to formulate rules of behavior reflecting the principle of reciprocity, including the need for sincerity, sympathetic insight, and sympathy, in seeking and attaining the goal of life, is a fundamental part of the science of ethics.

Additionally, men face the best ways of conducting their behavior in their relations with others. If we call this "morality," to distinguish it from the just-mentioned "ethics," morality includes not only polite etiquette but also conformity to mores and customs and abiding by the laws of one's society. All this is related to what Confucius called *li,* the appropriate way of expressing one's intentions in his overt social behavior. Rituals of one's family, community, and nation, and ways of memorializing one's ances-

When Confucius became discouraged about making little progress in playing the five-stringed lute, his teacher, Shang, encouraged him, saying that nevertheless he had captured the spirit of the music.

tors and heroes—all of these are a part of this same morality.

Finally, religion, which is man's concern for his ultimate values, or his actual quest in seeking to attain the goal of his life, somehow encompasses all of the other activities of his life and gives them direction. Philosophy of religion has as its task the understanding of the nature of religion. Confucius' concept of *chih,* wisdom, which is not mere understanding, but also full commitment to unwavering endeavor to attain the goal, is the key ideal in his religion. *Chih* is a man's discovery of and assent to the need for being completely honest, both with himself and with others, regarding wanting what is best for all. Having achieved *chih,* or even having only begun to achieve *chih,* a man then lives confidently, serenely, and generously, because he knows that he is embodying nature's way, *tao* and *teh,* and *yi, jen,* and *li,* and *chung* enduringly in his living. That is, when one combines the results of the sciences, including the social and psychological sciences, and of ethics and morality, in both discovering and then pursuing persistently the purpose of his life in accordance with them, then one is living religiously. Only as one becomes completely willing to do things the best way, and fully devoted to this purpose, when one is with others as well as when alone, and overtly as well as inwardly, can he be said to be fully religious. Such undeviating devotion to good will for all is what constitutes genuine living, *chung yung*.

Misunderstandings Although the uninitiated reader may need no warning about misinterpreting works which can speak for themselves, certain misinterpretations have become almost traditional as a consequence of the biased perspectives of earlier Western investigators. Presupposing that philosophy must consist in metaphysics, epistemology, and logic, some Western interpreters viewed Confucian moralizing as lacking in philosophy. Those who regarded the doctrines of Lao Tzu and Confucius as antithetical tended to overlook the fact that Confucius employed an intuitive type of epistemology, and accepted a non-Western kind of logic illustrated in the *I Ching*. It is unreasonable to expect that the philosophy of Confucius, formulated in the sixth century B.C., should be any more fully worked out than Greek or Hebraic philosophy of the same era. The fact that Chinese philosophy did not develop on Western lines is not, in itself, grounds for condemning it as being not philosophy.

More widespread, if not more serious, misinterpretations stem from the mistaken Western view that religion must be theistic and, therefore, Confucius was not religious. Insistent attempts by Western theists to discover and evaluate Chinese religion have led to at least five kinds of mistakes, namely, that Confucianism is not a religion, is agnostic about religion, is a religion of ancestor worship, is insincere animistic religion, is a religion deifying Confucius.

The view that Confucius was not religious stems from the mistaken view that, in order to be religious, one must believe in a God or gods. Now that Oriental studies have opened our eyes, we must recognize that the fact that Jainism and Theravada Buddhism explicitly denounce theism, for example, and that Hindu ideas of deity differ enormously from those in the West, requires us to have much broader conceptions of religion. Confucius was a naturalistic humanist for whom *Tao* (Nature) and *tao* (e.g., one's human nature) were sufficient metaphysical explanations and for whom the way to the goal, *chih,* incorporated all the other virtues with wholehearted commitment. In my opinion, the philosophy of Confucius expresses one of the noblest and wisest philosophies of religion.

The view that Confucius was agnostic about religion appears justified by his comment that, since we do not even understand life itself, how can we claim to know about life after death? It appears to be true that he was unconcerned about the existence of spirits. But again, the shallow view that religion is fear of spooks should not blind us to the magnificence of Confucius' confidence that Nature or Providence had supplied all that was needed to happily achieve his goal of life.

The view that Confucius advocated a religion of ancestor worship has a basis in his recommendations, and his own practice, regarding ways and manners of respecting departed ancestors. Reverence for ancestors was indeed a part of the harmonious way of life for Confucius. But his conclusions about such reverence flowed not only from his observations about the ways in which people in the happier kingdoms behaved but also from his understanding of the basic social principle of reciprocity. Answer the question for yourself: How do you wish to be treated when you become a departed ancestor? Do you desire to be forgotten immediately? Or do you hope to be remembered for some time, at least by those nearest and dearest to you? If you desire to be remembered in some way and for some time, then, according to the principle of reciprocity, ought you not then remember your departed relatives in the same way? After you are dead, do you want them to believe that you no longer exist in any way whatsoever, or do you hope that, somehow, their memory of you will still have some beneficial influence upon their lives? If so, then according to this same principle of reciprocity, ought you not also believe that your departed ancestors still have such a beneficial in-

fluence upon your life and that, thus, they have whatever kind of existence may be involved in having such
influence? If reverence for ancestors constitutes ancestor worship, then Confucius advocated it. But if
"ancestor worship" connotes belief in the substantial
existence of departed souls as hovering ghosts, then
there is certainly no need for it in the philosophy of
Confucius.

The view that Confucius practiced insincere animistic religion was expressed by Mo Ti, rival and
critic of Confucius. He claimed that Confucius was
inconsistent, not believing in the existence of spirits,
thereby displeasing them, while at the same time
advocating punctilious performance of ceremonies
designed to please them. Those who take spirit worship in earnest, as did Mo Ti, naturally see Confucian ceremonialism as insincere. But Confucius,
greatly concerned about sincerity, *hsin,* focused his
interest on interpersonal relationships. If there are
genuinely appropriate manners of behaving when
one pays his respects, *li,* then anyone who does believe in spirits should express his attitude sincerely
by employing the appropriate modes of behavior and
do so as perfectly as he can. That is, having discovered fundamental principles of association, Confucius could advocate that they be used in all social
circumstances. One who does not have an uncle may
still know how an uncle should be treated if he had

one. So, one who remains unconcerned about the existence of spirits may still know how spirits should be treated if there were, or are, any.

The view that Confucianiam is a religion because Confucius himself was later deified is founded on certain historical facts. Followers and admirers venerated him increasingly, and he was, finally, awarded the same ceremonial honors which the emperor performed annually for *T'ien*, Heavenly Providence. But there is no hint in the doctrines attributed to Confucius that he had any such interest or expectation, and, except for some enthusiastic devotees, proposals to deify Confucius were never seriously supported by the Chinese people. This view too, suffering from the mistaken notion that religion involves belief in deity, directs attention away from, rather than toward, the ideal of *chih* which epitomizes Confucius' conception of religion.

Hosts of other kinds of misunderstandings cannot detain us here. (I have treated these at some length in *The World's Living Religions,* pp. 191–95.) Persons committed to other ideologies tend to develop vested interests in depreciating Confucius. Buddhists, Jains, Hindus, Marxists, Freudians, Existentialists, Rationalists, and Sinophobes all can find reasons inherent in their own presuppositions for belittling Confucian ideals. I do not claim that the philosophy of Confucius is wholly adequate, because I believe that each philosophy has some truth to it and a wholly adequate philosophy will draw upon the positive resources which all of the other philosophies exploit. But I do claim that a person falls short of appropriating for himself the cultural riches of all the world's civilizations if he fails to understand and appreciate the profundity of the insights to be found in the writings associated with Confucius.

Concerning the Translated Texts In the texts that follow, together with the notes I have added, I am more concerned with accuracy and clarity than with paraphernalia. Hence I have made a few departures from the traditional arrangement of the texts: 1) The section headings and numbers are of my own devising, but a table of equivalents is given below for the convenience of those readers who may wish to consult other translations. 2) Sentence or paragraph numbers have been omitted. 3) Unnecessary "Confucius said" introductions to sentences have been omitted. 4) Phrases needed to state more fully implied meanings have been inserted in brackets. 5) As indicated in the notes, the opening sentence of Section 28 has been moved to a more appropriate place in Section 27.

For information concerning my methods of dealing

with translations, see the Acknowledgments at the end of the book.

The following tables correlate my section numbers (in Arabic figures) with those of the traditional versions (in Roman figures):

GENUINE LIVING

1=i	8=xiv	20=xxi	27=xxviii
2=ii–v	9=xv	21=xxii	28=xxix
3=vi–ix	10=xvi	22=xxiii	29=xxx
4=x	11=xvii	23=xxiv	30=xxxi
5=xi	12=xviii	24=xxv	31=xxxii
6=xii	13=xix	25=xxvi	32=xxxiii
7=xiii	14–19=xx	26=xxvii	

GREAT WISDOM

1=Intro.	4=iii	7=vi	10=ix
2=i	5=iv	8=vii	11–13=x
3=ii	6=v	9=viii	

Genuine Living
[Chung Yung]

♦ 1 ♦   Personal Source of Social Harmony

What Nature[1] provides[2] is called "one's own nature."[3] Developing in accordance with[4] one's own nature is called "the way of self-realization."[5] Proper pursuit of the way of self-realization is called "maturation."[6]

One's own nature cannot be disowned.[7] If it could be disowned, it would not be one's own nature. Hence, a wise man pays attention to it and is concerned about it, even when it is not apparent[8] and when it does not call attention to itself.[9]

One's external appearance[10] is nothing more than

---

1. *T'ien,* commonly translated "Heaven," here interpreted as Nature *(Tao)* in its initiating or providing (i.e., *yang*) aspect.

2. I.e., furnishes, brings about, causes to be, determines, or endows one with originality. When "Nature" is regarded as the "provider of all things," it may be called "Providence."

3. Lit., "what he is."

4. I.e., living in accord with, or following.

5. Lit., *tao,* the self-realizing, self-fulfilling way.

6. *Chiao,* education, in the sense of drawing out and developing one's natural capacities; or learning, in the sense of learning how to live by discovering what happens as one proceeds to fulfill his life.

7. Or abandoned, discarded. One cannot be separated from his own nature.

8. Lit., "invisible," hidden from view, or not obvious.

9. Lit., "inaudible."

10. I.e., visible exterior. Doubtless refers to appearance to others, and hence to one's self as public or social. Opposite of "not apparent" (see footnote 8).

an expression of his invisible interior,[11] and one's out-
ward manifestation[12] reveals only what is inside.[13]
Therefore the wise man is concerned about[14] his
own[15] self.

Being unconcerned about [attitudes toward others
and by others involving] feeling pleased, angered,
grieved, or joyful is called "one's genuine personal
nature."[16] Being concerned [about such attitudes],
each in its appropriate way, is called "one's genuine
social nature."[17]

This "genuine personal nature" is the primary
source[18] from which all that is social develops. This
"genuine social nature" is the means whereby everyone obtains happiness.

When our "genuine personal nature" and "genuine social nature" mutually supplement each other

11. Doubtless connotes private or individual self.

12. I.e., how one's self is extended or expanded through its
interests in others.

13. I.e., within the self as an individual.

14. Not worried or agitated, but devoutly attentive.

15. I.e., private or individual self.

16. *Chung,* genuine. Here interpreted as "one's genuine personal nature" for purposes of contrasting it with his additional
social nature.

17. *Ho,* genuine together; i.e., mutually sharing in helping
each to develop his own genuine nature.

18. Lit., "great root."

perpetually, then conditions everywhere[19] remain wholesome, and everything thrives and prospers.

• 2 • Difficulties in Self-Development

The wise man retains his genuine personal nature.[1] The foolish man does the opposite.[2]

A wise man is wise because he always retains his genuine personal nature, and the foolish man does the opposite because, being foolish, he fails to appreciate what is good.[3]

One's genuine personal nature is self-sufficient. But how few people can maintain it for a long time!

I know why the course of one's genuine personal nature is not pursued. Men of achievement try to surpass it. The inept fail to maintain it.

I know why the course of one's genuine personal nature is not understood. The ambitious overestimate it. The lazy fail to appreciate it.

19. Lit., "Heaven and earth."

1. I.e., "follows *teh*." When an individual does this he embodies *chung*.
2. I.e., "lacks *teh*." He wavers from, or deviates from, the way and dissipates his resources.
3. Just as wisdom and integrity mutually sustain each other, so folly and ignorance contribute to each other.

With some of his disciples, Confucius visited Lao Tzu in the land of Chou, both because the people of Chou were noted for their respectful manners and because the customs of Lu, Confucius' native state, had been inherited from them.

All men eat and drink. But there are few whose taste tells them when they have had precisely enough.[4]

Regrettable indeed is this failure to follow one's genuine personal nature.

◆ **3** ◆   **Some Can, Some Cannot**   Consider Shun, for example. He had great wisdom. He liked to inquire and to examine the views expressed, no matter how simple. He ignored what was bad and elicited what was good. By apprehending opposing extremes, he made clear the middle[1] way. Such was Shun's disposition.

Everyone thinks, "I am wise."[2] But being urged onward, they become ensnared[3] unawares. Everyone believes, "I am successful."[4] But even when they happen to follow their own true nature, they cannot persist in following it for a whole month.

4. Often translated as "Few know how to distinguish flavors."

1. I.e., genuine.

2. I.e., I comprehend Nature's way, my own genuine nature, and how to direct it prosperously.

3. Lit., caught in a web, trap, or well.

4. I.e., successful in comprehending and fulfilling one's genuine nature.

Consider Hui as an example. He chose to follow his genuine nature. When he perfected his behavior in any way, he stuck to it, appreciated it, and never departed from it.

One may be able to govern his country, his state, and his family perfectly, to forego honor and prosperity, and to risk death without hesitation,[5] without being able to realize his own genuine nature.

• 4 • Personal Virtue Exemplified

Tzu Lu inquired about virtue.[1]

Confucius replied: Do you mean "Southern virtue" or "Northern virtue" or the virtue which is best for you?

Southern people idealize patience and gentleness, readiness to help[2] others, without wanting to punish mistreatment. Southern gentlemen[3] embody these virtues.

---

5. Or to remain courageous in the face of drawn swords; or, perhaps, to suppress armed rebellion.

1. I.e., strength of character. Virtue in the sense of manliness, exhibiting enduring tendencies for reliability or the courageous qualities needed to meet and deal with social situations; not virtue in general.

2. I.e., teach.

3. I.e., the ideal man as measured by Southern standards.

Northern people admire readiness to fight and to risk death without hesitation. Northern heroes[4] emulate these virtues.

However, the wise man lives in harmony with others without being led astray by them. How wholesome is his virtue!

He establishes himself in the middle way without leaning toward either side. How intelligent is his virtue!

When propitious practices prevail in public affairs, he remains undeviating in his private life. How reliable is his virtue!

When vicious practices prevail in public affairs, he still retains his [virtuous] habits without modification even in the face of death. How enduring is his virtue![5]

◆ **5** ◆ **Pretension Is Unwise** To investigate the mysterious and to perform the spectacular for the sake of future reputation is something which I will not do.

4. I.e., brave men, or those regarded as ideal by Northern standards.

5. Our words, "wholesome," "intelligent," "reliable" and "enduring" are different renderings of the same Chinese symbol. Other translations include "firm," "steadfast," "unbending," "unflinching."

The wise man emulates Nature in all his ways. To do so in only some ways is not enough.

The wise man accepts his genuine nature. Even though he may be completely unknown, ignored by everyone, he lives without remorse. Only one who is saintly can do this.

♦ **6** ♦   **Nature's Way Is Sufficient**   Nature, which the wise man[1] emulates, is apparent everywhere but also hidden in each thing.

The most ignorant people have some knowledge of it, yet even the wisest of men cannot comprehend it fully. The most degenerate people embody it somewhat, but even the wisest of men cannot emulate it perfectly. [For] magnificent as the universe[2] is, man still wants it to be different.

So, when the learned man expresses his ideals of greatness, the actual world does not fully exemplify them. And when he expresses his ideals of minute distinctions, nothing in the actual world can embody them.

It is written in the *Book of Verses:* "The eagle soars high up in the sky and the shark dives down into the

1. *Chun tzu.*
2. Lit., "all in Heaven and Earth."

depths." This saying illustrates how Nature extends above and below.

*   *   *[3]

The [social] nature of the wise man originates from the simplest relations between men and women; it grows to full maturity, it comprehends everything in the world.[4]

♦ 7 ♦   Nature's Way Is Self-Correcting

Nature's way is not something apart from men. When a man pursues a way which separates him from men, it is not Natures's way.

In the *Book of Verses* it is written: "When one molds an axe handle, his pattern is not far away." The

---

3. Although the following sentence is grouped with the others in Legge's collection, its meaning appears to be of a different order. More probably it serves as an introduction to the theme of the following section. The foregoing deals with the idea of *tao* in general or as it is, or is not, fully embodied in an individual. The following section deals with the interrelations between people, or social relations; and this sentence reminds us of the ideals stated in the opening section about how happiness for the individual depends upon conducting his social relationships in accordance with the simplest Taoistic principles. Here we have one of the clearest statements of Confucius' reply to Lao Tzu's advice to shun association.

4. I.e., all that is needed for happiness.

model for the handle is in the hand which grasps it, [even though] when we compare them, they appear different. So likewise, the wise man influences men by appealing to their natures. When they revert [to nature's way], he stops.

When one develops his nature most fully, he finds that the principles of fidelity and mutuality[1] are not something apart from his nature. Whatever you do not want done to you, do not do to others.

The nature of a wise man includes four achievements, none of which I have attained: 1) To appreciate[2] my father as I wish my son to appreciate me. This I have not been able to do. 2) To serve my superior officers as I desire my subordinate officials to serve me. This I have not been able to do. 3) To treat my elder brother in the same way I would ex-

1. Both terms should be interpreted as having positive and negative aspects. Fidelity, or loyalty, involves good will toward others, positively, and desire to prevent evil, negatively. And mutuality, or reciprocal benevolence, includes willingness to be treated as we treat others, positively, and effort to refrain from treating others in ways in which we do not wish to be treated, negatively. C. C. C. Chang interprets negative mutuality as involving forgiveness and positive mutuality as involving conscientiousness.

2. The four terms "appreciate" (or "revere"), "serve," "treat," and "be considerate" are varied renderings of the same Chinese symbol, usually translated simply as "serve."

When Confucius was appointed Prime Minister of Lu, at the age of fifty-one, within three months he managed to eliminate crime, gained the confidence of the people, and established harmonious order throughout the land.

pect my younger brother to treat me. This I have not been able to do. 4) To be as considerate of friends as I would like to have my friends be considerate of me. This I have not been able to do.

[The wise man] is attentive to both his behavior and his speech. Whenever his behavior becomes deficient, the wise man tries to correct it. Whenever his speech becomes annoying, he restrains himself. Thus, while speaking, he gives constant attention to his actions, and, when acting, he gives constant attention to his speaking. Should not a wise man be thus constantly attentive?

◆ **8** ◆   **Humility Is Wise**   The wise man adapts himself appropriately to each situation. He does not desire to make it different.

When he finds himself amid wealth and dignity, he conducts himself as one who is worthy and esteemed.

When he finds himself among the poor and despised, he behaves in ways appropriate to poverty and disdain.

When he finds himself in a foreign civilization, he adapts himself to foreign customs.

When he finds himself in distress and affliction, he acts as one who is distressed or afflicted.

[Thus] the wise man is willing to accept every appropriate kind of behavior as his own.

When in a high position, he does not regard his inferiors with contempt. When in a low position, he does not flatter his superiors.

He [always] acts appropriately of his own accord, and needs no guidance by others. Hence, he does not feel himself imposed upon. He neither grumbles about his cosmic fate nor complains about his treatment by men.

Thus the wise man is serene and confident, trusting the future. But the foolish man risks troubles, hoping for more than he deserves. The wise man is like an archer. When the archer fails to hit the target, he reflects and looks for the cause of his failure within himself.

♦ **9** ♦   **Start at the Source**   The nature of a wise man is something like going on a long journey, since in order to go far he must first go through what is near, and is something like climbing a high peak, since in order to attain the top he must first start at the bottom.

In the *Book of Verses* it is written: "Happy association with wife and children is like the music of lutes and harps. When cordiality prevails among brothers, the harmony is pleasing and gratifying. With your household harmoniously organized, enjoy the companionship of your wife and children."

In such circumstances, parents enjoy contentment.

♦ **10** ♦ **Wisdom Is Invisible**   How profusely do invisible powers manifest their influence!

When we look for them, we cannot see them. Yet they are present everywhere, and nothing is without them.

They move masses of people to fast and to purify themselves and to bedeck themselves with their finest raiment in order to sacrifice to them. The world seems flooded with them, both above and on all sides.

In the *Book of Verses* it is written: "The invisible powers come upon us unawares. Yet they cannot be ignored."

Such is the way in which the invisible is expressed. And such is the impossibility of restraining expressions of faith.

◆ **11** ◆ **Wisdom Is Most Worthy**

How admirable was the considerateness[1] of Shun! He possessed the character of a wise man. He was worthy to be regarded as an emperor.[2] He owned everything in the whole world.[3] Memorial services were conducted in his honor in ancestral halls. And his memory was cherished by his descendants.

This illustrates how having such a character results in high position, great wealth, good reputation, and long life.

In this way, Nature, in creating all things, provides for them according to their capacities. Thus it nourishes that which is flourishing, and brings to its end that which is declining.

In the *Book of Verses* it is written: "The revered and gracious leader exemplifies illustrious character. He organizes his people and coordinates his officers. He benefits from Nature's providence. Nature protects him, helps him, and elevates him. Nature supports him continuously."

So it is that he who possesses a virtuous character will receive a high calling.[4]

1. Lit., "respect for parents," usually translated "filial piety."
2. Lit., "son of Heaven."
3. Lit., "everything within the four seas."
4. Lit., "receive an appointment as emperor," or a "Heaven-appointment."

◆ 12 ◆ Rewards of Wisdom Exemplified

It is said that only King Wen had no reason for sorrow. King Chi was his father and King Wu was his son. His father founded his high estate and his son perpetuated it.

King Wu preserved the high standard established by King T'ai, King Chi, and King Wen. Once he buckled on his armor, the empire became his. He maintained respect throughout the land. He dignified the realm. He owned everything in the whole world. Memorial services were conducted in his honor, and remembrance was cherished by his descendants.

King Wu was old when he came to the throne, and Duke Chou carried on the worthy traditions of Wen and Wu. He aggrandized the memorials to King T'ai and King Chi; he honored all of their ancestors with royal rites; and he augmented the honors awarded to princes, to officials, to scholars, and to ordinary people.

When a father was a higher official and his son was a lower official, the father's burial rites were those of a higher official and the son's memorial services were those of a lower official. But when the father was a lower official and his son a higher official, then the father's funeral services were those of a lower official and the son's memorial services were those of a higher official.

Mourning honors for high officials were extended for one year. Those for the emperor were extended to three years. But his etiquette decreed that mourning periods for the parents of people in both high and low ranks should be the same.

◆ **13** ◆ The Wise Are Considerate   How thoroughgoing was the filial considerateness of King Wu and Duke Chou!

Now filial considerateness consists in diligently fulfilling the desires of one's fathers and in perpetuating their achievements.

In spring and autumn they renovated the memorial halls, tidied up the ceremonial urns, aired the robes and vestments, and prepared offerings appropriate to each season.

First, they properly distinguished between ancestors of different generations and lines of descent when conducting memorial services for the family. Next, they treated honorees according to their rank, as having had high or low stations in life. Then, recognition was given to differences in worthiness of accomplishments.

When the ancestors were celebrated by a toast, persons of lower ranks presented the cup to their superiors. In this way, the lowliest persons were able

The people of Ch'i,
fearful of Confucius'
success as Prime
Minister of Lu, sent
eighty beautiful women
to the king of Lu.
When the king devoted
himself to carousing
with them and
neglected affairs of the
country, Confucius
resigned in disgust.

to participate. At the feast table, the elders were served first, ranking according to age.[1]

To occupy the same places which our fathers occupied, to perform the ceremonies just as they did, to play the same music which they played, to honor those whom they honored, to love those whom they loved; and to respect those who are dead as they were respected when alive and to regard the departed as still as worthy as if they were with us—this is the perfect exemplification of filial considerateness.

By performing the seasonal ceremonies, we pay our appropriate respects to the cosmic forces, and by performing memorial services, we pay our appropriate respects to our ancestral progenitors. He who comprehends the significance of the seasonal ceremonies and of the memorial ceremonies[2] is as fit to govern a kingdom as to care for his own hand.[3]

1. Lit., according to color of hair.
2. By which we accept the naturalness and propriety of the principle of reciprocity in relation to cosmic forces and to departed ancestors as well as to living beings.
3. Lit., palm.

♦ **14** ♦ Good Government Depends on Good Men Duke Ai[1] inquired about government.

Confucius replied: The reigns of Wen and Wu have been recorded. While such men ruled, good government prevailed; but when such men were gone, good government disappeared.

When good men are in office, government is efficient, just as when the earth is fertile, plants flourish.

Therefore, good government depends upon good men. Such men should be chosen on the basis of character. Good character is developed by following nature.[2] By following nature, one acquires good will.[3]

Good will is essential to being human, and it emerges first in caring for one's family. The best way of doing things[4] is to recognize each thing for what it is, especially for its true worth. Just as there are differences in the care with which we treat closer and more distant relatives, so we should recognize differences in merit for different levels of responsibility, and accept them in social practice.[5]

When those who are governed do not have confidence in their governors, they cannot be controlled.

1. Governor of Lu, where Confucius lived.
2. *Tao;* i.e., developed through growth of common sense.
3. *Jen.*
4. *Yi.*
5. *Li.*

Therefore a leader ought not to neglect the development of his own character. In endeavoring to develop his character, he should not fail to acquire an understanding of human nature.[6] By achieving an understanding of the nature of man, he does not fail to gain insight into Nature.[7]

◆ **15** ◆ **Social Relationships** The nature of social [i.e., mutual] relationships may be illustrated by five [social relationships], and the traits[1] needed to fulfill[2] them [may be summarized as] three.

The relationships are those 1) between sovereign and subject, 2) between father and son, 3) between husband and wife, 4) between elder brother and younger brother, and 5) between friend and friend

---

6. I.e., of how people behave in their relations with each other.
7. Lit., "Heaven."

1. I.e., qualities, capacities, characteristics, virtues, or good abilities.
2. No English word quite adequately expresses the idea of living in these relationships in such a way as to provide opportunity for realizing oneself and an obligation to make use of the opportunity and developing habits of enjoying such use, and thus bringing about a value-fulfillment in and through them.

associating as equals. These five exemplify the nature of all social relationships.[3]

3. (1) The relation between "sovereign and subject" illustrates all relations between higher and lower officials, no matter how high or low in the ranks of public offices or, for that matter, private corporations as they now exist. (2) The relation between "father and son" is a model also for mother and daughter, or for parents and children generally, and extends by analogy to grandfathers and great-grandfathers and to grandsons and great-grandsons, etc. (3) The placing of the relationship between "husband and wife" third in the list, or in the middle of the list, has caused much discussion. Some people regard this relation as the most intimate and would place it first. However, a child depends upon his parents for existence, his nourishment and protection, and moral lessons. Those who receive most care from their mothers may wonder why the mother-child relationship is not regarded as more significant and instructive. In a patriarchal family, it is the father who has the responsibility and who should be recognized as superior to his son. If obedience, rather than intimacy, is the criterion for gradations, then, while obedience to sovereign and father may be strict of necessity, the obedience of a wife to her husband may be less so. (4) The relation between "elder brother and younger brother" serves also as a model for elder sister and younger sister, for relations between older cousins and younger cousins, second cousins, aunts, uncles, etc. (5) The relationship between "friend and friend associating on an equal basis" may provide insights which can be used not only for relations between intimate friends but also for less intimate friends, remote acquaintances, temporary guests, and even enemies. Since the Confucian principle of reciprocity requires a person to treat every other person as he would like to be treated if he were that person, i.e., to treat his father as he would like to be treated if he were his father and his son as he would like to be treated if

The three traits—concern *(chih)*, good will *(jen)*, and conscientiousness *(yung)*[4]—are required in all social relationships. In effect, the way in which these [three] traits function is unitary.[5]

Some persons seem born with social aptitudes.

he were his son, the fifth relationship, which specifies equality, has a significance for moral instruction which is somewhat different from those in which one finds himself in superior-inferior relationships.

4. *Chih*, i.e., willingness, attentiveness, readiness, and devotedness to discovering ways in which one can care for the needs of others. Note that, elsewhere, we have interpreted this term as "wisdom." *Jen*, i.e., willingness to have each other person attain and maintain his own welfare and happiness. The Taoistic ideal depicts each person as attaining happiness through following his own genuine nature. So both of the first two traits require one to seek insight into the peculiar nature of each person he is concerned about. *Yung* or "conscientiousness" here involves the ideas of having confidence, faith, or trust ("courage" or "bravery") that being concerned and having good will for all is the best and of feeling guilty ("having shame") when failing to have such confidence or when failing to do one's best in exercising the care needed.

5. Although the three may be distinguished for discussion, in practice they must function together. One does not feel concern at one time, good will at another, and exhibit conscientiousness at still another. Without all three acting together, the capacity for associating wholesomely is diminished. Neither can bring about the desired result alone. Furthermore, all three must be guided by the spirit of genuineness and, indeed, it is this spirit which demands all three.

Some acquire them by learning from teachers. And some develop them through trial-and-error experiences. But no matter how obtained, they operate in the same way.

Some persons express their concern for others spontaneously, some by calculating the rewards in prospect, and some by reluctantly forcing themselves. But when concern [and good will and conscientiousness] for others is expressed, then [regardless of whether they are expressed spontaneously, calculatingly, or reluctantly] the results are the same.

To be fond of learning[6] is close to having wisdom *(chih)*. To try hard is close to having good will *(jen)*. To have feelings of guilt contributes to conscientiousness *(yung)*.

When a person understands these traits, then he knows how to develop his character. When he knows how to develop his character, then he knows how to guide others. When he knows how to guide others, then he knows how to govern the whole country, including its states and communities.

6. Not learnedness, but learning how to live in the best way.

After departing from Wei, Confucius went to Cheng. Despite his divine inspiration and sagely wisdom, the people there treated him like a vagabond.

◆ **16** ◆ **Nine Practical Principles**   Whoever
is responsible for governing the whole
country, including its states and communities, has
nine principles to practice:

1. The development of his own character.
2. Recognition of those who are worthy.
3. Expressing due affection for his relatives.
4. Having complete confidence in his most responsible officials.
5. Taking a personal interest in the problems of
all other public officials.
6. Paternal treatment of the common people.
7. The fostering of manufacturers and tradesmen.
8. Gracious entertainment of foreigners.
9. Appreciating the services of political leaders.[1]

When a governor develops his own character, he
thereby secures the operation of Nature's way *(tao)*[2]
in his realm.

When he recognizes those who are worthy, he
avoids the evils of favoritism.

When he expresses due affection for his relatives,
they will have no reason for complaint.

When he has complete confidence in his most

1. Lit., governors of states.
2. I.e., the best, healthiest, most wholesome way of conducting government which is in accordance with the "*tao* of
society" or the principles of social science.

responsible officials, he will refrain from meddling in their affairs.

When he takes a personal interest in the problems of all other public officials, he earns their personal gratitude.

When he treats the common people with a paternal attitude, then their morale improves.

When he fosters manufacturing and trade, the country will prosper.

When he entertains foreigners graciously, people from everywhere will be attracted to him.

And when he appreciates the services of political leaders, then the whole country remains loyal to him.

◆ 17 ◆ How to Become a Responsible Leader

By self-restraint, cleanliness, neatness in dress, and refraining from all inappropriate behavior, this is the way for a leader to develop his character.

By ignoring slander, remaining unresponsive to enticements, disregarding riches, and acknowledging accomplishments, this is the way to recognize those who are worthy.

By respecting their positions, helping them to become well off, and sympathizing with their preferences, this is the way to express due affection for one's relatives.

By giving them a free hand and full authority to carry out their duties, this is the way to have complete confidence in the most reliable officials.

By assuring them of job security and providing them with good salaries, this is the way to take a personal interest in the problems of all other public officials.[1]

By requiring public celebrations only on regular holidays and lowering their taxes, this is the way to improve the morale of the common people.

By daily supervision and monthly inspections to insure fair wages and just prices, this is the way to foster manufacturers and tradesmen.

By greeting them upon arrival and escorting them when they depart, and by praising their proficiency and forgiving their inexperience, this is the way to entertain foreigners graciously.

By restoring to honor the families of former governors, by reinstating control in states where the government has collapsed, by re-establishing order in states which have become chaotic and by protecting those who are in danger, by conducting councils [of representatives of the states] at regular intervals, by requiring them to bring in only small assessments

1. Today Confucius would speak here of "civil servants."

and sending them away with large appropriations, this is the way to appreciate the services of political leaders.

These, then, are the nine principles for successful practice for all who have to govern a country or a state or a community. Success results from using all of them in the spirit of genuineness.

♦ **18** ♦ **Preparation Pays** In all affairs, achievement depends upon previous preparation; without such preparation, failure is certain. When one decides beforehand what he wants to say, then his speech will not falter. When he determines beforehand how he wishes to deal with things, he will not meet trouble later. When one plans his course of action, he will not become perplexed. When one employs the best ways of proceeding *(tao)* habitually, then he will profit from them perpetually.

When those who are governed do not have confidence in their governors, they cannot be controlled.[1]

[But] there is a way for a governor to gain such confidence:

1. See section 14.

[First, he should recognize the principle that] if he cannot be trusted by his friends, then he will not be trusted by those whom he governs.[2]

There is a way to gain the confidence of one's friends: [One should recognize the principle that] if he is not faithful to his parents, then he will not be trusted by his friends.

There is a way to be faithful to one's parents: [One should recognize the principle that] if he is not honest with himself, then he cannot be faithful to his parents.

There is a way to be honest with oneself: [One should recognize the principle that] if he does not know what is good,[3] then he cannot be honest with himself.

• 19 • Man's Way Versus Nature's Way

Nature's way[1] is to *be* genuine.[2] Man's way is to *become* genuine.

2. Or, if he has a superior sovereign, he will not be trusted by him.
3. I.e., best for himself.

1. Lit., "way of Heaven."
2. "Genuine" here is the same word as "honest with himself" in section 18.

To be genuine is to act truly without effort, to attain without thinking about it, and automatically and spontaneously to realize one's genuine nature. Such a man is wise.

To become genuine is to try to do what is good and to keep on trying.

In order to do this,[3] one must first thoroughly investigate the nature of what is good, earnestly inquiring about it, meticulously examining it, clearly formulating a conception of it, and diligently learning from practical experience with it.

So long as there is anything[4] which he has not investigated, he will not cease in his efforts.

So long as there is anything which he has not thoroughly examined, or anything in what he has examined which he does not understand, he will not cease in his efforts.

So long as there is anything of which he has not formulated a clear conception, or anything in such a conception which he does not understand, he will not cease in his efforts.

So long as there is anything which he has not tried out in practical experience, or anything in such experience which he does not understand, he will not cease in his efforts.

3. I.e., to choose what is good and cling to it.
4. I.e., about the nature of what is good, etc.

While journeying to visit Chao Chian-tzu, Confucius learned that Chao had murdered two friends to whom Chao was deeply indebted for his success. Thereupon Confucius condemned Chao as an unjust man and discontinued his journey.

Even though others may succeed with a single effort, he will put forth a hundred efforts [if necessary], and where others succeed with ten attempts, he will make a thousand attempts [if necessary].

Whoever follows this way, even though he be sluggish, he will achieve understanding; even though he is weak, he will attain strength.

♦ 20 ♦ Two Sources of Genuineness

When our understanding springs from our genuineness, it may be said to emerge from our nature.[1]

When our genuineness is derived from our understanding, it may be said to result from education.[2]

From genuineness we may develop understanding and from understanding we may acquire genuineness.

1. I.e., it may be called "instinctive."
2. Here we have an ancient formulation of the "nature-nurture controversy."

♦ **21** ♦ **How to Influence the World** It is only he who is completely genuine in the affairs of this world who can develop his own nature to its fullest.

If he can develop his own nature to its fullest, then he can help in the full development of the natures of other men.

If he can help in the full development of other men's natures, then he can help in the full development of the natures of all animate and inanimate beings.

If he can help in the full development of all animate and inanimate beings, then he can help in the production and maturation activities of Nature above and Nature below.

When he helps in the production and maturation of Nature above and Nature below, he likewise becomes a creative agent in the universe.

♦ **22** ♦ **Hope for the Partly Genuine** Next[1] is he who develops genuineness only partially. From this, he can experience [the nature of] genuineness.

1. I.e., in addition to him who can develop his nature to its fullest.

In this way, [the nature of] genuineness becomes actualized [in him].

When it becomes actualized [in him], then it becomes apparent [to him].

When it becomes apparent [to him], then it becomes clear [to others also].[2]

When it becomes clear [to others also], then it influences them.

When it influences others, they are molded by it.

When they are molded by it, they are improved.

It is only he who is completely genuine in the affairs of this world who can improve others.

· **23** · Achieving Predictive Power It is natural[1] for a completely genuine man to be able to predict [the course of things].

When a nation or a family is about to become prosperous, evidences of good [tendencies] are certain to appear, and when it is about to become ruined, evidences of evil [tendencies] appear.

They[2] can be seen both in external means of

2. Lit., it shines forth.

1. I.e., is a consequence of following nature *(tao)*.
2. I.e., the evidences of these tendencies.

prognostication[3] and in how they affect one's bodily behavior.[4]

When ruin or prosperity is in prospect, he can surely foresee both good and evil outcomes. Therefore, the completely genuine man is like one having superior powers.

◆ 24 ◆ Genuineness Improves Both Self and Others Genuineness is self-sufficient. And its nature is self-directing.

Genuineness pervades being from beginning to end. Without genuineness, nothing could be done. This is why the wise man values becoming genuine above everything else.

The person who tries to be genuine not only promotes [his own] self-realization. He also promotes the self-realization of others.[1]

Self-realization involves associating with others

3. Lit., in the milfoil and the lines on the shells of tortoises, methods commonly employed in Confucius' day. For further insight into the orthodox system for organizing various kinds of evidence, see the *I Ching*.

4. Lit., affect the movements of the four limbs.

1. Lit., "things."

(jen). Developing one's relations with others involves sympathy.[2] Both associating with others and having sympathy are abilities which anything has for realizing its own nature *(teh).*

One's whole nature *(tao)* integrates both external[3] relations and inner[4] processes. Hence, genuineness is fully genuine when both of these abilities are appropriately integrated.

◆ 25 ◆ Genuineness Is All-Pervading

Therefore, what is most genuine pervades everything without ceasing.

Being unceasing, it is everlasting. Being everlasting, it is self-sufficient.

Being self-sufficient, it is all-inclusive. Being all-inclusive, it extends everywhere and is self-sustaining. Extending everywhere and being self-sustaining, it ascends high and shines forth.

By extending everywhere and being self-sustaining, it contains[1] everything. By ascending high and

2. Which includes developing sympathetic insight.
3. I.e., social, or relations with others.
4. I.e., individual.

1. I.e., like a receptacle, holding things together from below.

shining forth, it covers² everything. Being all-inclusive and everlasting, it brings [all] things to their completion.

By extending everywhere and being self-sustaining, it appears³ as the [whole] earth. By ascending high and shining forth, it appears in the heavens. By being all-inclusive, it is without limit.⁴

Such is the nature of genuineness. Even though it is invisible, it produces [all] changes. Even though it exerts no effort, it accomplishes everything.

The nature *(tao)* of Nature⁵ may be summed up in one word: "genuineness." It is free from duplicity.⁶ How it does what it does is a mystery.

The nature of Nature⁷ is such that it extends everywhere and is self-sustaining, ascends high and shines forth, and is all-inclusive and everlasting.

That bit of heaven which appears above us now is only the visible portion of the sky. But when thought

2. I.e., like a tent or house which spreads over it and encloses it from above.

3. Lit., it pairs with, or is equal to.

4. I.e., there is nothing outside it or beyond it.

5. Lit., the nature of Heaven and Earth.

6. I.e., deceit, or being one thing and wanting to, or trying to, or pretending to, be another. The universe and the things in it are what they are. He who refuses to accept what is as it is, is self-deceived and a deceiver of others.

7. Lit., the way of Heaven and Earth.

When traveling on the road from Chen to Tzai, Confucius learned of two wise scholars who had turned recluses and become farmers. He went to obtain information from them, but they refused to give it, saying they did not care what happened to the rest of the world. Confucius remarked sadly: "Do not those who have received knowledge know that they have a duty to share it with others?"

of as unlimited, encompassing the sun and moon, stars and galaxies, it overarches everything.

This bit of earth here under us is but a handful of dirt. Yet when considered in its breadth and depth, it supports heavy mountains[8] without strain and retains rivers and oceans without letting them drain away.

This mountain here before us looks like a mere pile of rocks; yet on its broad slopes grow grass and trees, birds and animals make their homes on it, and stores of valuable minerals abound within it.

This lake here before us seems like a mere dipperful; yet in its bottomless depths swim myriads of fishes and turtles and sharks.[9] Bountiful resources swarm within it.

In the *Book of Verses* it is written: "The provisions of Heaven! How plenteous and unfailing!" This means that such [plenitude and endless supply] is what makes Heaven Heaven.[10]

Also, "King Wen's ability to follow nature unwaveringly *(teh)*! How excellent!" This means that such [ability to follow nature unwaveringly] is what made King Wen King Wen. Unwavering pursuit need not end.

8. Lit., mountains like Hwa and Yoh.
9. Lit., large tortoises, iguanas, iguanodons, dragons, fishes, and turtles.
10. Or, such is the nature of Nature.

◆ **26** ◆ Superiority of the Sage. How superior the nature of sageliness!

Bountiful as the ocean, it can stimulate and inspire all living beings, and ascend to the heights of Heaven.

How proficient [is] its superiority!

It masters all of the principles of propriety and all of the rules of etiquette.[1]

It awaits the right man, and then it becomes actualized.

Hence it is said: "Unless one has the ability to follow nature *(teh)* completely, nature *(tao)* cannot function perfectly."

Therefore, the wise man prizes his ability to follow nature without deviation *(teh)*. He persists in self-examination and inquiry [into the needs of others], trying to pursue it to its fullest breadth, yet giving attention to its finest details, and striving to develop it to its highest excellence. In this way he develops his genuine self *(chung yung)*. This is the reason why he both studies ancient history and is alert to the latest news. He is genuinely interested in both respect for and practice of whatever is right *(li)*.

So, while holding a high position, he is not haughty, and when he finds himself in a low position, he does not complain.

---

1. Lit., the three hundred rules of ceremonies and the ten thousand rules of conduct.

When social conditions are naturally wholesome *(tao)*, his advice is admired. When social conditions become disorderly,[2] he is tolerated if he maintains his silence.

Is not this the significance of the *Book of Verses* when it says: "By wisdom and discretion he perpetuates himself"?

◆ 27 ◆ Ability Needed for Responsibility

One who is uninformed and yet opinionated, one who is incapable of caring for himself and yet wants to have his own way, and one who faces present problems and yet refuses to profit by past experiences—all such people are courting disaster.

Only the emperor[1] has the capacity to establish proper procedures *(li)*, to fix weights and measures, and to prescribe linguistic usage.

2. Lit., deviate from nature's way *(tao)*.

1. Lit., Son of Heaven, connoting not merely the highest political authority but also the person with the broadest perspective and greatest insight. If Confucius were writing today in a complexly interdependent society, doubtless he would urge heeding the counsels of committees of experts instead of the chief executive.

Today, throughout the country, we enjoy standardized parts for machines,[2] uniform script for all writing and printing, and common customs.

He who becomes ruler of the country must regulate [these] three important matters, if he would prevent mistakes.[3]

If one occupies a position of responsibility[4] but lacks the necessary capacity, he ought not revise the established procedures or standards of taste.[5] If one has the capacity but lacks the position of authority, he cannot revise the system of procedures or artistic standards.

I can report the customs *(li)* of the [ancient] Hsia kingdom, but [the usages still persisting in the contemporary state of] Ch'i are insufficient evidence of them. I have investigated the customs of the [ancient] Ying[6] kingdom, and they still prevail in the [contemporary] Sung state. I have learned the customs of the Chou kingdom, which prevail today. I follow these.

2. Lit., wheels of carriages are all of the same size.
3. This sentence, which introduces section XXIX in the traditional sequence, appears more properly to belong here.
4. Lit., the throne.
5. Lit., make music.
6. Or Shang.

◆ **28** ◆ How a Sage Generates Confidence[1]

No matter how excellent the ancient customs, [if they cannot be tried out today, their value] cannot be demonstrated. Without demonstration, people will not follow them.

No matter how excellent the moral advice coming from those who lack prestige, it will not be respected. Without such respect, people will not have faith in them. Without such faith, people will not follow them.

Therefore, the regulations promulgated by a sagely leader should be founded upon his own character and experience, and [they should be] adequately demonstrated in the lives of the people. They should be verified historically[2] to see whether they are deficient. They should be correlated with cosmic principles[3] to see whether they are consistent with them. They should be displayed before departed ancestors without fear or hesitation. They should be felt worthy of scrutiny by sages centuries later, without any uncertainty.

By displaying his regulations before departed ancestors without fear or hesitation, he demonstrates his knowledge of Heaven. By being willing, without

1. The opening sentence of this section has been moved into the preceding section (see note 3 above).
2. Lit., compared with those of the three kings.
3. Lit., accord with Heaven and Earth.

feeling uncertain, to await the scrutiny of sages centuries later, he demonstrates his knowledge of men.

When this is so, then the deportment of the leader serves as a model, his conduct is regarded as a standard, and his language serves as an example before the whole country for generations. Those who are distant from him admire him, and those close to him never tire of him.

In the *Book of Verses* it is written: "Without animosity there, without boredom here, day after day, night after night, they recite his praises."

No wise man, without earning such laudation, ever became famous throughout the ancient world.

♦ 29 ♦ Magnificence of Nature's Way

Confucius transmitted the teachings of Yao and Shun[1] as if they were his own ancestors, and expounded the precepts of Wen and Wu, and eulogized them. They harmonized with the reliable rhythms of heaven above,[2] and were consistent with the regularities in the earth and water below.

In their inclusiveness and sustainingness, and in

1. Ancient emperors.
2. I.e., day and night, the seasons, changes in the weather, etc.

After finishing his writings about the classics, Confucius performed a ritual to the Big Dipper. When a ray of light shone down and traced a gemlike inscription on the altar, he took the phenomenon as a good omen that his work would be handed down forever.

their comprehensiveness and protectiveness, they are comparable to Heaven and Earth.

In the orderliness of their procedures, they are comparable to day and night[3] and the four seasons.

[They teach how] all things flourish together without harming each other. Each thing follows its own nature *(tao)* without interfering with others. Lesser things such as rivulets [follow their own courses, while at the same time] greater processes [such as day and night and the four seasons pursue] their tremendous transformations. This is why Nature[4] is so magnificent.

· **30** · **The Sage Has Depth and Breadth**

Only the most sagely person in the world can unite in himself the quickness, clarity, breadth, and depth of understanding needed for guiding men, the magnanimity, generosity, benevolence, and gentleness needed for getting along with others, the attentiveness, strength, stability, and tenacity needed for maintaining control, the serenity, seriousness, unwaveringness, and propriety needed

3. Lit., to the sun and the moon in taking their turns at shining.
4. Lit., Heaven and Earth.

for commanding respect, and the well-informedness, methodicalness, thoroughness, and penetration needed for exercising sound judgment.

Because he exercises his abilities when they are needed, he is able to do all kinds of things, to serve wide areas, to penetrate deeply, and to flow on perpetually.

In being able to do all kinds of things and to serve wide areas, he is like Heaven. In penetrating deeply and flowing on perpetually, he is like the ocean. Whenever he appears, everyone adores him. Whatever he says, everyone trusts him. Whatever he does, everyone is grateful to him.

Consequently, his fame spreads throughout the country and extends to foreign lands. Wherever carts and boats go, wherever human enterprise penetrates, wherever the sky reaches and the earth extends, wherever the sun and moon shine, and wherever the frost and dew settle—all who live and breathe honor him. For this reason, it is said: "He is equal to Heaven."

◆ **31** ◆ **The Sage Is Whole-hearted**   Only the most completely genuine man in the world is able to harmonize the opposing strands of human society, to establish and maintain moral order in the country, and to understand the develop-ing and maturing processes of Nature.[1] Need such a person depend upon anything outside himself?

How whole-hearted his good will!

Who can comprehend such a man unless he him-self has quickness, clarity, breadth and depth of understanding, and breadth of perspective?

♦ **32** ♦ **The Sage Is Humble**   In the *Book of Verses* it is written: "Over her ornate gown she wears an ordinary dress," implying dislike for ostentation. Similarly, it is the nature of a wise man to refrain from ostentation, while gaining in renown daily; whereas it is the nature of the foolish man to seek notoriety, while gaining disrepute daily.

The wise man does not appear exciting, yet people never become bored with him. Although seeming simple, he is really intricate. Although apparently friendly, he remains serious. He knows that attain-ment of distant goals comes through attentiveness to things near at hand. He knows the causes of things.[1]

1. Lit., Heaven and Earth.

1. Lit., from where the wind blows.

He knows how little things grow into big things. Such a person embodies a sound character.

In the *Book of Verses* it is written: "That which is deep and foundational may still be quite apparent." Therefore the wise man scrutinizes his inmost self, to eradicate evil and to eliminate inadequacy. That in which the wise man is unexcelled cannot [fail to be] seen by other men.

In the *Book of Verses* it is written: "Even when secluded in privacy, be free from guilt, for you are visible in light from above." Therefore, the wise man continues to have high regard for good behavior even when he is inactive, and for truthfulness even when he is silent.

In the *Book of Verses* it is written: "One worships in silence,[2] without resentment."[3] Therefore, the wise man does not offer enticements, and still the people are uplifted. He does not express anger, and yet they are moved more than if threatened with hatchets and clubs.

In the *Book of Verses* it is written: "Good character does not need to be advertised. Noble men seek it anyway." Therefore, when the wise man remains genuine and attentive, the whole world attains peace.

2. I.e., he does not speak out and ask for favors in return for his homage or sacrifice.

3. I.e., if no reward is forthcoming.

In the *Book of Verses* it is written: "I admire your excellent character. How unpretentious—neither loud nor showy." Among the means of influencing people, loudness and showiness are least effective.

Again in the *Book of Verses* it is written: "Character is as unobtrusive as a hair." Yet even a hair can be obtrusive in some degree. "The actions of Heaven are without sound or odor." That is perfection.

Great Wisdom
[Ta Hsueh]

♦ **1** ♦   **The Essence of Wisdom**   Great wisdom consists in fully perfecting intelligence,[1] in restoring morale to the people, and in attaining the highest good.[2]

To know what is best is to determine one's goal. To determine one's goal is to steady his aim. To steady his aim is to proceed with assurance. To proceed with assurance enables one to conduct his life with insight. By conducting his life with insight, one reaches his goal.

Things have their order.[3] Events have their sequence.[4] To know what is proper in order and natural in sequence is to approach the truth. Those

1. "Intelligence" *(teh)* is the ability to attain the goal of life. For an extensive treatment of the meaning of *teh,* see pp. 86–92 of my edition of *Tao Teh King by Lao Tzu.* See also "Meanings of Intelligence," *Philosophical Studies,* vol. XIV, 1955, pp. 151–55. The phrase *chai min min teh,* translated as "to clear clear virtue" by Constant C. C. Chang and as "to illustrate illustrious virtue" by Legge, refers, apparently, to full and complete embodiment of *teh.* One has achieved great wisdom only when the ideal of achieving *teh* is exemplified in his living to the fullest extent possible.

2. Lit., "to stop at the best." I judge this phrase to have two aspects: First, one is wise only if he refuses to stop until he has achieved the best. Second, one is wise only if, when he attains what is best, he refrains from going farther—since the only way to go farther is to depart from what is best, or to deviate from Nature's way.

3. Lit., their roots and their branches.

4. Lit., their beginnings and endings.

ancients who desired to set an example of good character for everyone[5] first established moral order in their states.

In order to establish such order in their states, they first guided their families.

In order to guide their families, they first developed themselves.

In order to develop themselves, they first had to acquire a right attitude.

In order to acquire a right attitude,[6] they first tried to become honest with themselves.

In order to become honest with themselves, they first had to learn as much as possible.

Learning as much as possible involved gaining insight into the nature of things.

By gaining insight into the nature of things, they came to know the highest good.

By apprehending the highest good, they became honest with themselves.

By becoming honest with themselves, they acquired the right attitude.

By acquiring the right attitude, they developed themselves.

By developing themselves, they guided their families.

---

5. I.e., for the whole world. Lit., all places under Heaven.
6. Or get into a right mind.

By guiding their families, they established moral order in their states.

By establishing moral order in their states, they brought peace and prosperity to the whole country.

From the highest official to the ordinary people, all need to recognize that self-development is fundamental.

When the fundamentals[7] are neglected, what is developed from them cannot be sound. It is unreasonable to neglect the important and to devote oneself to the trivial.

♦ **2** ♦ **Historical Examples** In the *Letter to K'ang* it is written: "King Wen succeeded in making his character exemplary."[1]

In the *Tai Chia* it is written: "King T'ang constantly observed the exemplary prototype of Nature."[2]

In the *Ti Tien* it is written: "King Yao succeeded in making his character fully exemplary."

All these [three kings] made themselves exemplary.

7. Lit., the root.

1. Or in achieving perfect intelligence (as stated in the opening sentence of section 1 above).
2. Lit., Heaven.

When Confucius was
ill, his disciple Tzu
Kung went to visit him.
He found Confucius
leaning against his
gatepost and lamenting:
"Why must great
mountains crumble!
Why do sages have to
die!" Seven days later
he was dead—at the
age of seventy-three.

♦ 3 ♦ Need for Recreation

On King T'ang's bathtub were carved the following words: "If you can recreate yourself in one day, then do so every day. Yes, there should be daily recreation."[1]

In the *Letter to K'ang* it is written: "Recreate the people anew."

In the *Book of Verses* it is written: "Although Chou was an old state, its life was perpetually renewed."[2]

Therefore, the wise man always tries to do his best.

♦ 4 ♦ Happiness the Goal

In the *Book of Verses* it is written: "The goal of the country[1] is the happiness of the people."

In the *Book of Verses* it is written: "The chirping

---

1. Lit., renewal. "Recreation" here means not entertainment, sports, or physical exercise but rather revitalization of intelligence in the sense of returning from deviations back to the middle way. In the opening sentence of section 1 above, this term was interpreted as "restoring morale." The renewal is both individual and social, as outlined in section 1.

2. Lit., always received new guidance from Heaven.

1. Lit., the imperial domain of a thousand *li*.

yellowbird is happy in the corner of a hill." If the bird knows how to be happy, ought a man know less than a bird?

In the *Book of Verses* it is written: "How admirable was King Wen! How exemplary his character! How much he appreciated the happiness of his realm." As a king, he was happy when good will *(jen)* prevailed. As an administrator, he was happy with propriety. As a son, he was happy with respecting his father. As a father, he was happy in kindness to his son. When speaking to the people of the country, he was happy in being truthful.

In the *Book of Verses* it is written: "Behold the meandering river of Ch'i. How green and lush its bamboo trees! Here is our graceful and talented Prince! He has been carved and filed and chiseled and polished! How serious and dignified! How majestic and commanding! Our graceful and talented Prince can never be forgotten."

The words "carved and filed" refer to studying hard. "Chiseled and polished" refers to the development of his character. "Serious and dignified" refers to his cautious and considerate attitude. And "our graceful and talented Prince can never be forgotten" means that when a character has achieved complete maturity and the highest good, the people will not forget it.

In the *Book of Verses* it is written: "The ancient kings, Wen and Wu, are not forgotten." Gentlemen still admire what they admired and like what they liked. And the common people are pleased with them and profit from their benevolent provisions. This is why these ancient kings are not forgotten.

◆ **5** ◆ **Prevention Better Than Cure**   In judging[1] disputes, I do what anyone else would do.

What is needed is to prevent people from having disputes. By preventing wrongdoers from succeeding,[2] men's minds are conditioned to fearing [to act wrongly].

This is called "understanding fundamentals."[3]

1. I.e., arbitrating.
2. Or by demonstrating that "crime does not pay."
3. Lit., knowing the root.

◆ 6 ◆ Foundations and Fulfillments[1]

The foregoing[2] is called "understanding the fundamentals."[3]

The following[4] is called "the fullness of understanding."[5]

◆ 7 ◆ Avoiding Self-Deception

What is meant by "keeping our purpose genuine" is to prevent self-deception. We should hate what is evil[1] and love what is good.[2] This is called "appreciating one's own nature." Hence, the wise man guards his intentions even when he is alone.

1. The body of this section, according to Chinese tradition, is a commentary by Chu Hsi, which is commonly omitted from English translations and which is not included here. Chu Hsi (A.D. 1130–1200) rearranged an earlier edition to form the order in the present edition. An account of this rearrangement is to be found in C. C. C. Chang's *Story of Chinese Philosophy*, chs. I, XXII.
2. The foregoing sections 2–5, including the latter part of section 1.
3. Lit., "knowing the root."
4. The following sections 7–11.
5. Or fulfillment.

1. Lit., bad odor.
2. Lit., beautiful view.

The foolish man, when he is alone, thinks he can get away with anything.[3] But when he encounters the wise man, he is embarrassed. He tries to hide his evil intentions and pretends to have good ones. Yet, since whoever watches him sees through his pretensions, what does he gain? This illustrates the saying that "whatever really is inside has a way of expressing itself."[4] This is why the wise man guards his intentions when he is alone.

Master Tzeng remarked: "What everyone notices[5] and calls to the attention of others,[6] should be regarded seriously."

When goodness pervades one's abode, then his mind becomes expansive and his body relaxed. Therefore, the wise man keeps his intentions genuine.

♦ **8** ♦   **Emotion Distorts Judgment**   What is meant by saying that "self-development depends upon maintaining the right attitude"[1] is this:

3. Lit., is free to do any evil he likes.
4. I.e., "Truth will out."
5. Lit., "what ten eyes see."
6. Lit., "what ten hands point to."

1. Lit., "on being in the right mind."

When a person becomes enraged with anger, he cannot control himself properly. When he becomes overwhelmed with fear, he cannot remain objective. When he becomes enthralled by love, he cannot maintain proper perspective. When he becomes submerged in sorrow and grief, he cannot preserve a balanced view.

When our mind is unattentive, we look without seeing, listen without hearing, and eat without tasting.

This is what is meant by saying that "self-development depends on maintaining the right attitude."

• 9 • Prejudice Hinders Development

What is meant by saying that "the proper guidance of one's family depends upon the development of one's own self" is this:

People are biased in their attitudes toward those whom they love, toward those whom they hate, toward those to whom they feel superior. Therefore, few people in the whole world can see the faults in those whom they like or the virtues in those whom they dislike.

Hence, as we commonly say, "Parents cannot believe that their own children are really bad, and

After they had buried
Confucius, his disciples
mourned beside the
grave for three years
and then went about
their business. But Tzu
Kung stayed on for yet
another three years.

先聖墓

the farmer cannot believe that his crops will not be bountiful."[1]

This is what is meant by saying that "if a man's self remains undeveloped, he is incapable of guiding his family properly."

◆ 10 ◆ Guiding Family Prepares for Governing State

What is meant by saying that "in order to establish moral order in his state, one must first guide his family properly" is this:

One cannot convince others of what he cannot convince the members of his own family of. Therefore the wise governor does not need to go beyond his family in torder to find the principles needed for governing his state. Here he finds his own son's respectful obedience[1] to his father, with which a governor should be served, affection for one's relatives,[2]

---

1. Thomé H. Fang summarizes this proverb as follows: "Biased lovers are blind and greedy people can never be satisfied."

1. Usual translation: "filial piety."
2. I.e., elder brothers, uncles, etc.

with which higher officials should be treated, and paternal kindness, with which all people should be regarded.

In the *Letter to K'ang* it is written: "Behave as if you were watching over an infant." A mother, in caring for her child, may not be able to do exactly what is needed, but she comes close to doing so. A girl does not need to learn how to suckle a baby before she marries [and has one of her own].

When good will prevails in one family,[3] it influences the whole country, and when courtesy prevails in one family, the whole country becomes courteous. On the other hand, the selfishness and rudeness of one man[4] can cause turmoil throughout the whole country. This is the way things work. This confirms the saying that "one slur can poison the whole atmosphere; one hero can inspire a whole country."

[Kings] Yao and Shun guided the country through good will, and the people emulated them. [Kings] Chieh and Chow ruled the country with violence, and the people emulated them. When their edicts differed from what they themselves practiced, the people did not comply. Therefore, a leader must first embody in himself the qualities which he wishes

3. I.e., the governor's.
4. I.e., the governor.

to instill in others; and he must first purge from himself any qualities which he wishes to eliminate from others. No one who fails to regard others like himself is able to improve them.

Therefore, the government of a country depends upon appropriate guidance of the family.

In the *Book of Verses* it is written: "The peach tree, how lovely! How beautiful! How rich in blooms! The bride goes to her husband's home, and exercises guidance over her family." When the family has been properly guided, then the country can be wisely governed.

In the *Book of Verses* it is written: "They treated their elder brothers properly. They treated their younger brothers properly." After a ruler has treated his elder and younger brothers appropriately, then he is ready to serve as a model for the country.

In the *Book of Verses* it is written: "His conduct is ideal. He serves as a model for everyone."[5] When a ruler becomes a model father, son, and brother, then the people will emulate him.

This is what is meant by saying that "the establishment of moral order in the state depends upon properly guiding the family."

5. Lit., "the four states."

◆ ‖ ◆ Wisdom Prerequisite for Wealth

What is meant by saying that "by establishing moral order in their states, they brought peace and prosperity to the whole country" is this:

When the ruler respects his elders as elders should be respected, then the people will respect their elders. When he treats his seniors as seniors should be treated, then the people will learn to respect their superiors. When he is charitable to the poor and weak, the people will not do otherwise.

Thus the wise ruler has a principle[1] which serves him as a standard[2] with which to guide his conduct:

Whatever one dislikes in those above him he should not present to those below him, and whatever one dislikes in those below him he should not present to those above him. Whatever one dislikes in those in front of him he should not present to those behind him, and whatever he dislikes in those behind him he should not present to those in front of him. Whatever one dislikes in those on his right he should not present to those on his left, and whatever one dislikes in those on his left he should not present to those on his right.

1. Lit., *tao.*
2. Lit., "a measuring square."

This is what is meant by [saying that] "*tao* serves as the standard for guiding his conduct."[3]

In the *Book of Verses* it is written: "How admirable is the wise ruler who takes a parental attitude toward his people."[4]

In the *Book of Verses* it is written: "How majestic is the Southern Mountain! How awesome are its rugged rocks! How majestic is the great preceptor Yin! How much people admire him!" The ruler of a country must not fail to be careful; for if he does fail, disaster will follow.

In the *Book of Verses* it is written: "Before the rulers of the Yin dynasty lost the allegiance of the people, they were regarded as equal to the gods. Behold the Yin![5] A position of great trust is not easy to maintain." This implies that by winning the people the country is won, and by losing the people the country is lost.

For this reason a wise ruler will be concerned first about his own character. By achieving character, he wins the people. By winning the people, he obtains [control over] the land. By obtaining the land, he

3. Here is one way of formulating the principle of reciprocity, or the Confucian "golden rule." I prefer to call this principle "the *tao* of society."

4. Lit., "is a father and mother to his people."

5. I.e., as an example.

acquires wealth. By acquiring wealth, he attains power to influence.

◆ 12 ◆ Wealth Depends on Character

Character is fundamental; wealth is a consequence.[1]

When one treats fundamentals as secondary and consequences as primary, then he incites discord and encourages fraudulence among the people.

So by gathering wealth[2] one fails to acquire [the allegiance of] the people; and by failing to gather wealth [first] one acquires [the allegiance of] the people.

Therefore, when a ruler speaks improperly, he will be spoken to improperly. And when wealth is gained by unfair means, it will be lost in the same way.

In the *Letter to K'ang* it is written: "Positions of trust are not eternal." This means that worthy behavior begets trust and unworthy behavior begets distrust.

1. Lit., character is the root; wealth is the branch.
2. I.e., first, before achieving character, or by attending to consequences first before fundamentals.

In the centuries since his death, Confucius has been honored by memorial ceremonies without number. Depicted here is a ceremony performed by a Han emperor two centuries after his death.

In the *Book of Ch'u* it is written: "The state of Ch'i does not regard things as important. It regards worthy men as important."

Fan[3] remarked: "Those who have been exiled do not regard things as important. Good will toward fellow men is what they regard as important."

In the *Book of Ch'in* it is written: "Had I but one minister who is simple and honest! Having no abilities other than good will and habits of doing what is best, he would appreciate the abilities of others as he would his own, so that when he found a man of experience and intelligence, he would admire him inwardly more than he expressed through words of praise, thus demonstrating genuine appreciation of him. Such a man would protect my children and my descendants and all of the people.[4] Such a man would be a great asset to the country.

"But when a minister is jealous of the abilities of other men, he dislikes them. When he finds a man of experience and intelligence, he will hinder him and prevent his advancement, thereby demonstrating his lack of appreciation of him. Such a man would be unable to protect my children and my descendants and all of the people. Such a man would be dangerous."

3. Uncle of King Wen.
4. Lit., "sons, grandsons, and the black-haired people."

Only a man of good will can ostracize such a man, expelling him from civilized society,[5] exiling him to barbarous lands. This illustrates the saying that "only a man of good will is competent to approve or disapprove other men."

⋅ **13** ⋅ **Wisdom Requires Discretion** To recognize a person as worthy without honoring him with a high position, or to honor him without doing so soon enough, this is being deficient in appreciation. To recognize an unworthy person without dismissing him or to dismiss him without banishing him,[1] this is being lacking in courage.

To like what people dislike and to dislike what people like is contrary to human nature. Misfortune will befall whoever does so.

Hence, there are naturally[2] fundamental principles of rulership. One must follow them faithfully and earnestly in order to succeed. If one becomes proud or immoderate, he will fail.

There is a superior way to increase wealth. When the producers are many and the consumers are few,

5. Lit., from the Middle Kingdom.

1. Lit., "without sending him sufficiently far away."
2. I.e., in accordance with *tao*.

and when there is much concern about production and frugality in consumption, then wealth will always be sufficient.

The wise man uses his wealth to improve himself. The foolish man uses himself to increase his wealth.

There never has been a situation in which a ruler liked to express good will *(jen)* and the people did not like to reciprocate *(li)*. There never has been a situation in which the people liked to reciprocate and the public business was not carried out fully. And there never has been a situation in which there was objection to the wealth of such a state being in the ruler's warehouses.

Master Men Hsien once said: "Those who attend to horses and carriages do not watch out for chickens and pigs. Those who tend to stores of ice do not herd cows and sheep."

So likewise, those who are wealthy rulers[3] should not employ tax collectors. For it is better that a ruler be robbed[4] than to employ a tax collector.[5] This is what is meant by saying that "the improvement of a state does not consist in improvement in prosperity, but in reciprocity."

3. Lit., the house which owns a hundred carriages.
4. I.e., by people failing to pay taxes.
5. Traditionally, tax collectors kept a large percentage of the taxes they collected. The temptation to engage in extortion and fraudulent reporting tended to be irresistible.

When a ruler's chief interest is in acquiring wealth, he must be under the influence of some base man[6] whose guidance he [mistakenly] believes to be good. But so long as he rules, misfortune and reprisals occur. Even after a good ruler replaces him, he cannot restore the damage.

This [also] demonstrates the saying that "The improvement of a state does not consist in improvement in prosperity, but in reciprocity."

6. I.e., one with low moral development, or lacking in *teh*.

Bibliography

Works consulted during the preparation of this volume:

Bahm, Archie J., *Tao Teh King by Lao Tzu*, Frederick Ungar Publishing Co., N.Y., 1958

Collie, David, tr., "Ta Heo" and "Chung Yung" in *The Chinese Classical Work Commonly Called the Four Books*, Mission Press, Malacca, 1828

Greenlees, Duncan, tr., from the French work of J. P. G. Pauthier, *The Gospel of China* (containing "The Great Study" and "Abiding in Poise"), Theosophical Publishing House, Adyar, Madras, 1949

Hillier, C. B., tr., "The *Ta-Heo*—The Great Lesson of Life" in *Transactions of the China Branch of the Royal Asiatic Society, Part III, 1851–52*, Office of the China Mail, 1853

Hughes, E. R., tr., *The Great Learning* and *The Mean in Action*, E. P. Dutton and Co., N.Y., 1943

Legge, James, tr., *The Great Learning* and *The Doctrine of the Mean* in *The Chinese Classics*, Vol. I, Oxford University Press, London, 1893

Lin Yutang, tr., "*Chung Yung* (Central Harmony)" and

"*Tahsueh* (Ethics and Politics)" in *The Wisdom of Confucius,* Random House, N.Y., 1938

Lyal, Leonard A., and King Chien-kun, trs., *The Chung-Yung or The Centre, The Common,* Longmans, Green and Co., Ltd., London, 1927

Marshman, Joshua, tr., "*Ta-Hyoh* of Confucius" in *Elements of Chinese Grammar,* Mission Press, Serampore, 1814

Morrison, Robert, tr., "*To-hiu:* the Great Science" in *Horae Sinicae; Translations from Popular Literature,* Black and Parry, London, 1812

Pound, Ezra L., tr., "Confucius: *The Unwobbling Pivot* and *The Great Digest*" in *Pharos,* No. 4, Winter, 1947

Acknowledgments

In accordance with the purpose of this volume, which is to gather up the key ideas of the philosophy of Confucius and to present them as clearly and systematically as possible for persons unacquainted with his views, three kinds of sources need to be recognized. The first: translations by others. The second: critical advice by Chinese scholars. The third: my own interpretation.

Translations used in editing the two interpreted texts differ for each of the works. In preparing the manuscript for the *Chung Yung* initially, I relied primarily on the works of Legge, Hughes, Collie, Lin, and Lyal, somewhat in that order. Pound's unrestrained use of poetic license and Greenlees' addiction to imaginative additions rendered these works practically useless. For deriving my edition of the *Ta Hsueh*, I depended mainly upon Legge, Hughes, Collie, and Lin. The works by Greenlees, Hillier, Marshman, Morrison, and Pound proved useless.

Critical advice from two Chinese scholars was obtained, first during a four-week visit to Taiwan, China, and later by correspondence. My initial manuscript interpreting the *Chung Yung*, prepared over several years, was almost complete when I arrived, but most of the work on the *Ta Hsueh* was done in Taipei. For repeated consultations, critical evaluation, and many corrections

during preparation of the manuscripts, I am indebted to
Professor Constant C. C. Chang (Chang Chi-chun) of
Taiwan Normal University. For penetrating discussion,
critical scrutiny of the completed manuscripts, further
corrections, and his kind Foreword to this book, I am
indebted to Professor Thomé H. Fang, Taiwan National
University, author of *The Chinese View of Life*. Neither
of these persons is responsible for the final version, and
some passages may not meet with their approval. I am
indebted to the United States Educational Foundation
in China for making my visit to Taiwan and consulta-
tion with these scholars possible.

Preparation of an edition expressing my own interpretation has seemed worth-while for both negative and
positive reasons. Negatively, (a) too many literalistic
translations are rendered with a wooden quality and
yield little significant meaning, especially about the
spirit of the whole. (b) Each of the translators has
adopted his own vocabulary, and some of the earlier,
perhaps better, translations employ a language less suited
to the idiom of today. (c) Some quite clearly reveal a
philosophical bias which was foreign to the thought of
Confucius. Greenlees interprets him as a rationalist, and
Lin as a theist, for example. (d) Some take undue lib-
erties in supplying imaginative embellishments which
appear misleading. The rendering of *Chung Yung* as "unwobbling pivot" seems not only false but also silly, thereby misusing the expression of a profoundly significant
philosophy as a poetic toy.

Positively, my studies in comparative philosophy
have led me to maximize the importance of systematic
wholes. Regardless of actual authorship, there is a philosophy, associated with Confucius, in which the ideas

fit together into a consistent whole. Even though the meanings of some original calligraphs have been lost in history, there is a system gestalt which can be grasped and, by ignoring the peculiarities of both ancient courts and contemporary American philosophies claiming that sentences and life are meaningless, we can find a core of key ideas which summarize certain kinds of experience which appear common to all mankind. My interpretation, too, is selective. Its aim is to introduce American readers to a great philosophy which can be grasped with clarity, simplicity, and wholeness. The need for understanding of, and sympathetic insight into, the philosophies emerging in other civilizations is very great. The wisdom attributed to Confucius constitutes a part of the cultural riches of mankind. I trust that readers will not lose sight of its wholeness, and wholesomeness, when they pursue their studies of Confucius in greater detail. The *Chung Yung* and *Ta Hsueh* have been selected, in place of the more famous *Lun Yu (Analects)*, a miscellaneous collection of sayings, because they do succinctly summarize its key ideals.

Finally, I am indebted to Clark Melling for bibliographical assistance, to Chien-sung Wu for translating and interpreting the Chinese captions to the Ming-dynasty prints used as illustrations, and to the Frederick Ungar Publishing Company for permission to quote extensively from my edition of the *Tao Teh King by Lao Tzu.*